Show Jumping

The author commentating at the White City, July 1967.

SHOW JUMPING

by

DORIAN WILLIAMS

FABER AND FABER
24 Russell Square
London

First published in mcmlxviii
by Faber and Faber Limited
24 Russell Square London WC1
Printed in Great Britain by
Latimer Trend & Co Ltd Plymouth

Standard Book Number 571 08543 1

Acknowledgements

Thanks are due to the following for permission to use their photographs:
Universal Pictorial Press for the frontispiece; Keystone Press Agency Ltd. for plates 4a & b, 10, 13, 14, 15; the Sport & General Press Agency Ltd. for plates 9a & b, 12b, 17a, 18a; the *Daily Mirror* for plates 15, 17b and 20; Peter Roberts for plate 18b and John Stonex for all the others.

Contents

Illustrations

Introduction

For a sport that was virtually unknown twenty years ago show jumping has a very considerable following. There are over 6,000 registered horses and ponies competing in the 2,000 or more horse shows held in Britain each summer. There is a viewing audience that can be as high as ten million.

The levels of interest, however, are extremely diversified, ranging from the ooh! and the ah! of the entirely uninvolved viewer to the meticulous professionalism of a Harvey Smith or Marion Coakes. A book entirely right for the one is going to be entirely wrong for the other, and vice versa.

As I see it, however, there are three groups involved in the sport to a greater or lesser extent, two of which can be brought sufficiently close for a single book to have a common interest.

The first group, of course, consists of the top riders. Although, like any other top athletes, they are always interested in new theories, new ideas, the very fact that they have reached the top or are approaching it, suggests that they have grown beyond the stage when a book, theoretical or instructional, can be of any great use to them, unless it is a rare work by an accepted master. Their interest in a book on show jumping, therefore, is purely academic, a cursory glance through to see if there is anything of fringe interest, crass stupidity or personal criticism.

This book obviously is not for them.

The second group consists of the very considerable numbers, mostly as one would expect young, who have comparatively recently taken up show jumping or are intending to do so, who welcome a little basic, straightforward advice, to support their

INTRODUCTION

own practical experience: something that they can consult, and then put into practice. In addition it is likely that they welcome a simple breakdown of the rules and regulations, and being human may also like to know something of the general background, including the historical, of the sport on the threshold of which they now find themselves.

Certainly, it is hoped, this book is for them.

The third group consists of that large number of people who do not ride, are never likely to, have never owned and will never own a horse, and yet, through in the first instance television, have become interested in show jumping: sufficiently interested what is more, to feel themselves considerably involved, anxious to know more about those taking part, the rules, the truth or otherwise of accusations of malpractices in training, the costs, the best type of horse, the prizes, the amateur status argument and so on.

I know this to be so from the large numbers of letters I receive after every television coverage of a big show. It is not just the usual so-called 'fan mail'—which is just as likely, incidentally, to be 'brick-bat' mail!—but people genuinely interested in writing to ask for enlightenment on some point.

This book, though there is a certain amount of mildly technical material, is, I hope, very much for them.

Any sport, indeed any activity, becomes so much more interesting the more that one knows about it. I hope, therefore, that this book may help people, both the active and the passive participators, to get increased enjoyment out of the sport of show jumping.

CHAPTER I

The Background

Few sports have developed so quickly from something virtually unorganized, enjoyed only by an exclusive few, to a sport with an administration second to none and an enormous popular appeal.

At the beginning of the century there was practically no show jumping except, in a limited way, in military circles. Even at the first International Horse Show held at Olympia with great splendour in 1907 show jumping played a very secondary part. It was the harness classes that were the great attraction.

It is generally believed that it was in Paris at the end of the last century that a jumping competition was first organized. The title *show* jumping was tagged on to it in order that it might not be confused with ordinary jumping out hunting or jumping in training for the *militaire*, the endurance test that has now become our Three-day Event.

In the years preceding the First World War show jumping was introduced at most military establishments where there were horses; and gradually horse shows, which in those days consisted principally of harness classes, began to introduce jumping classes.

But there were no set rules, nor established methods of judging. It was all very haphazard as was demonstrated when one of the earliest winners of the *Daily Mail* Cup, then the supreme individual award of show jumping at Olympia, won allegedly with a clear round but in fact fell off between the last two fences. In those days the chief judge would send an assistant down to mark each fence, but as there was no assistant between the last two fences the fall did not collect any faults!

It was only in 1921 that, due to the efforts of a number of cavalry officers, a set of rules were brought into being. Led by two young officers, both of whom were to become famous in the horse world, Col. 'Taffy' Waelwyn, father of the famous equestrian sculptress, and Col. V. D. S. Williams, my own father, they founded the British Show Jumping Association, the chief object of which was to draw up rules which could easily be understood by competitors, judges and even spectators.

The Association soon grew in influence and the standard of jumping quickly improved. Certain names became familiar in country circles and could be guaranteed to draw a crowd at any local agricultural show: Tommy Glencross, Miss Bullows—now Lady Wright—Sam Marsh, Tom Taylor, Phil Blackmore, Fred Foster, after whom a cup for one of the most important competitions at the Horse of the Year Show is named, Frank Alison.

But although these civilian riders could hold their own against the best of the military riders such as Malise Graham, Joe Dudgeon, Talbot Ponsonby, Howard Vyse, Dick Friedberger, Mike Ansell, de Fonblanque—I name them without their titles as in their jumping days they were considerably less senior than after the Second World War—yet they were never able greatly to distinguish themselves in international compeitions. Indeed although our military teams were successful both in England and on the Continent, and even on one occasion in the United States, they usually failed as individuals when they were riding against foreign competitors.

This was because of a slight but important difference in the rules drawn up by the British Show Jumping Association and sister organizations on the Continent. Whereas time scarcely entered into it in this country, abroad they insisted on a time limit. This was partly to make the jumping more of a test, partly to make it a better spectacle for the onlookers.

British riders unused to going against the clock, and indeed never trained to do so, found themselves at a disadvantage when competing against riders who were used to this style of riding. British riders were perfectionists, but lacked the dash of their foreign rivals, with the result that no civilian rider from this country had ever won an international competition up to the time of the Second World War.

The British public is fickle, and though it did not doubt that our horsemen were the best in the world, or that we bred the best horses, it found our endless international defeats disappointing and so, less than twenty years after this sport's revival through the founding of the British Show Jumping Association, the public became disenchanted: and though it is hard to believe this today, many of the bigger agricultural shows did not even bother to include a jumping competition in their programme.

It must have seemed to many in 1939 that show jumping was a thing of the past. By the time the war was over it would be a forgotten sport: in any case the likelihood was that there would be no place for equestrian sports in post-war Britain, except, of course, racing.

The truth could not have been more opposite. There was a hard core of enthusiasts who believed in the future of show jumping: a number of them were all in the same Prisoner-of-War Camp at Spanenburg, Oflag IX A/H. These included Col. Mike Ansell, Col. Nat Kindersley, and Col. Bede Cameron. The three of them combined to give talks to their fellow prisoners of war on show jumping—show jumping pre-war, show jumping post-war. They led discussions, and in a camp which included many from cavalry regiments, men who had been jockeys, trainers, hunt servants, had run riding schools, had ridden all their lives, it was understandable that the standard of discussion was high, and productive.

When in 1944 the prisoners of war were repatriated no time was lost in injecting new life into the skeleton British Show Jumping Association. With Col. 'Taffy' Walwyn as President and Col. Mike Ansell as Chairman the Association quickly proved itself to be high-powered and resourceful. They had two main objects: to improve the standard of jumping, which had, understandably, with the exception of such as Ted Williams, already in a class of his own, and 'Curly' Beard, sunk very low: and secondly to revive the public's interest.

Somewhat adventurously they decided to stage a Victory Show Jumping Championship in London. After various vicissitudes it was arranged to hold the Championship at The White City, the headquarters of the Greyhound Racing Association, to give a first prize of £100, the largest prize ever offered at that time, and to limit the entrants to those who had won more than £100 in jumping competitions.

The course was designed with great care, based on the research that had emanated from all the discussions in Spanenburg. For the first time in England a course was being built on scientific lines. The gorse hurdles and white poles, dumped down more or less anywhere in a figure of eight, were replaced by brightly coloured fences, the poles gaily painted, and to ensure that the horses really *saw* them, were packed with flowering shrubs, pot plants, and even oil drums: horses will never bother to jump flimsy fences that hardly merit a glance.

Distances between fences were carefully measured to coincide with the average length of a horse's stride. There were subtle 'changes of direction' to make sure that the skill of the rider was properly tested and that a horse could not just gallop round, virtually uncontrolled. The result was that not only was the course more impressive from the rider's and horse's points of view, but it was also far more attractive to the spectators.

Many of the riders, however, were somewhat sceptical. One or two diehards went so far as to withdraw their entries: they believed the fences to be unjumpable. They knew nothing, of course, of the deliberations in Oflag IX A/H, nor of those held later at the B.S.J.A. They were merely of the opinion—and some of them were frank enough to admit it—that the course designers had taken leave of their senses.

Most of the better known names in show jumping, however—Tom Taylor, Ted Williams, Curly Beard, Wilf White, Phil Blackmore—were all keen to have a crack at this new style course; and before long most of the more sceptical were prepared to admit that they had never known horses to jump better, more boldly or with greater ease.

The gamble had paid off. Theory in a prisoner-of-war camp in Germany in 1942 had been justified by practice at the White City in 1945; but an ending as romantic as a fairy tale caught the imagination of the crowd, in particular of the directors of the G.R.A. This was to affect profoundly the whole story of show jumping.

It can be truthfully said that the event that afternoon of 1st September 1945 was to start a chain of events that was to lead to Olympic Gold Medals and the highest prizes in show jumping.

With three more horses to jump in the jump-off of the Victory Championship it seemed that Ted Williams had it in the bag. His best horse, Umbo, had only half a fault, incurred by displacing the thin slat that in those days was laid along the top of the poles: a slat down cost half a fault, whereas if the whole pole came down it was four faults. Close behind Umbo were two more of Ted Williams' horses, Huntsman and Leicester Lad.

Then in came an 18-year-old chestnut called Maguire. He was an ex-Army horse, had jumped for the army before the war. In 1941, along with all the army horses, on the mechanization of the cavalry he was sold. The wife of his soldiering owner bought him—for £40!—knowing that her husband would like to think of his old friend happily retired in his own paddock, rather than sold to a new owner.

Towards the end of the war he started jumping again and qualified for the Victory Championship. It was the wife who rode him because his owner was a prisoner of war.

It was none other than Col. Nat Kindersley, from Oflag IX A/H. On repatriation he was reunited with Maguire, and now it was a clear round to win, in the Victory Championship.

All went well until he met the gate which was high off the ground, the absence of a well-defined ground line therefore making it particularly difficult; and he met it so completely wrong that he could not help but stop. This obvious incurrence of three faults for a refusal came as such a disappointment to the crowd when victory seemed within grasp that a great groan went up.

I have always thought that Macguire heard that groan for suddenly he propelled himself into the air like a helicopter. He seemed almost to climb the gate, and although when Maguire landed on all fours the other side the gate was swinging, shaking, vibrating, bouncing, rattling and shuddering, it never fell down; and Maguire had achieved a clear round.

A fairy tale ending indeed, and one that can never have been even considered in the dark days of 1942 in a German prisoner-of-war camp, when Col. Kindersley was one of the original speakers on show jumping of the future, one of those who led the discussions, confident that somehow show jumping would be reborn, even if personal triumph of the scale just recounted was never envisaged.

Col. Kindersley is now frequently Team Manager when British riders compete abroad.

Unfortunately fairy tales often introduce a sad note. This one is no exception, for the one man who would never get any personal enjoyment from riding over the new style fences was the one who had designed them all, whose drive and genius had made the dream a reality. Col. Mike Ansell had been blinded when taken prisoner at St. Valery in 1940, and though his sight was not to go completely for another three or four years he already had only one-tenth vision in one eye, and riding therefore was out of the question.

But what he lacked in physical sight he more than made up for with mental vision, and convinced after the Victory Championship that show jumping with a popular appeal and a high standard—sufficiently high to compete internationally—was possible, he wasted no time in putting jumping on the map.

That he, and the British Show Jumping Association, owed a great deal to the Greyhound Racing Association cannot be denied. After the Victory Championship Mr. Frank Gentle, Chairman of the G.R.A. at that time, sent for Col. Ansell and told him that though he knew little about horses he had for the last half hour of the competition found himself greatly excited.

He had been sitting on the edge of his chair: he had jumped every fence with every horse: his brow was perspiring, the palms of his hands were clammy.

'If all this can happen to me', he said, 'it can happen to thousands.'

He was convinced that show jumping could be a popular sport. To back his judgment he told Col. Ansell that if the International Horse Show could be revived at the White City, instead of at Olympia as before the war, the G.R.A. would be prepared to back all their losses for three years.

It was thus that the White City became the venue of the Royal (since 1957) International Horse Show, and the opportunity to use this magnificent stadium for this great show played a not inconsiderable part in the acceptance of show jumping by the general public. It was also a fine arena to which to invite foreign riders.

The presence at the top of a man of the calibre of Col. Mike Ansell quickly attracted to the sport people who might otherwise have been content with hunting and racing: in particular Col. Harry Llewellyn. Second in the Grand National on Ego, he might well have dedicated himself exclusively to racing after the war, but fortunately much of his great energy, skill, and not a little of his wealth was at the disposal of show jumping.

He bought a great horse, Kilgeddin, and a super horse, Foxhunter. These were to be the spearhead of our international revival. Indeed it was on Kilgeddin, in Rome 1947, that Col. Llewellyn won the first British international success.

A few weeks later the new International Horse Show at the White City was to see for the first time the combination of Llewellyn and Foxhunter that was to revolutionize show jumping: it was also to see another remarkable personality, at this time only eighteen, riding a horse called Finality, only 15 hands high. This was the début of Pat Smythe, whose own remarkable story—a girl with a simple background, learning to ride on Wimbledon Common, the Pony Club, orphaned before she was twenty, beating the best in the world before she was twenty-one, first lady to ride in the Olympics—and win a bronze medal—

was to fire the imagination of thousands of youngsters, who would not rest until they could take up riding and show jumping themselves.

Led by Harry Llewellyn our team, the other members of which were Col. Henry Nicholls on Kilgeddin and Col. Arthur Carr on Monty, won the bronze medal: a remarkable achievement when one remembers that only a year before had a British rider ever won an international event. Even more remarkable when one appreciates the fact that the gold and silver medals had been won by Mexico and Spain, two countries that had been spared full involvement in the war that had ended only three years earlier.

Four years later Britain did better still, winning the gold medal at Helsinki. The team, consisting of Llewellyn and Foxhunter, Wilf White and Nizefela and Col. 'Duggie' Stewart on Col. Llewellyn's great Irish-bred mare Aherlow, started hot favourites being virtually unbeaten in the Nations' Cup—team competitions—during the two preceding years; but a rare lapse by Foxhunter in the first round nearly put us out of it. However, at the fifty-ninth minute of the eleventh hour a superb clear round by Foxhunter clinched the matter: only the second clear in a hundred rounds. He had more than atoned for his lapse.

The year 1952 being a lean Olympic year for Britain—apart from Miss Altweg's medal in the Winter Olympics no British competitor won a medal of any sort—the last-minute gold suddenly made the press and public aware of a sport in which the British could succeed. Almost at the same time television had realized that show jumping was a sport that was particularly effective on the screen, and so quite suddenly Foxhunter and Nizefela, Tosca and Craven A and others became household names.

The interest was maintained throughout the success of our riders internationally. At Geneva every event was won by Britain. Foxhunter won his third King George V Cup at the White City—the most coveted individual international trophy in the world: the first horse ever to do so. Pat Smythe was the European Ladies Champion.

THE BACKGROUND

At the Olympic Games in Stockholm in 1956 we were in the medals again. In the team event we won the bronze, Nizefela coming fourth in the individual. Pat Smythe on Flanagan and Peter Robeson on Scorchin were the other members of the team. Also in 1956 we won five of the six Nations' Cup in which we competed. The fact that no less than ten different riders represented Britain in international teams stressed the strength of our position. We now had an almost bottomless reservoir of young riders good enough to represent their country.

Our team, though good enough to have won another medal, came unstuck at Rome in 1960, but David Broome on Sunsalve saved the day winning the bronze medal in the individual event, following it up with a victory in the European Championship: a feat emulated two years later by David Barker on Mister Softee (a horse to win the King George V Cup in 1966 for David Broome who in 1967 won the European Championship on it).

The pre-Olympic years saw our riders in tremendous form and at the beginning of 1963 a victory at Tokyo seemed more than a possibility. However, mishaps to our best horses resulted in Britain only being represented by a good rather than a great team, and we could do no better than fourth. Again at the eleventh hour, however, we snatched a medal when Peter Robeson won the individual bronze medal on Firecrest.

The following year Britain was back in top form. There were two new championships from which nations all over the world were invited to compete. The first was a Ladies World Championship which was won by Marion Coakes on her brilliant 14·2 h.h. Irish-bred pony, Stroller. The other was the President's Cup, offered for competition by Prince Philip, President of the International Federation, for the team winning most points in Nations' Cup: virtually a world championship. This, too, was won by Britain, drawing on no less than sixteen different riders to represent them.

Any chance of repeating this success in the President's Cup a year later, 1966, was eliminated when due to the swamp fever restrictions on the Continent it was neither possible for British riders to visit the Continent nor for riders from abroad to come

THE BACKGROUND

to Britain; hence we were not involved in any international competition, though Anneli Drummond Hay's victory in the Toronto Grand Prix on Merely-a-Monarch, competing against the best from Canada and the United States, reminded us of our potential as we approached the next Olympics.

From all of which it will be seen that show jumping has come a long way since the B.S.J.A. was founded in 1921. Originally the Association started with a hundred members. There are now 8,500, of which some 6,000 are competitors. Of these no less than 2,000 are juniors, reminding us of our strength in this section, our junior team having won the European Junior Championship every year but one since 1952.

There can be no doubt that it has been the success of our riders internationally and the success of the sport generally that have fired the imagination of so many young people to take up the sport, hoping that they too can reach the top, that they too can jump for Britain and win, perhaps, an Olympic medal.

But how easy is it? Just what are the difficulties with which the aspirant is faced? Just how great are the problems that have to be overcome? What are the priorities for horse and for rider? What are the qualities demanded?

CHAPTER II

Type of Horse

Again and again one is asked what is the right type of horse for show jumping. So often people think that because a racehorse has to be a thoroughbred, because a Welsh pony is ideal for a child's pony, because a hackney is right for harness, so a particular breed of horse is best suited for jumping.

Unfortunately this is not at all the case. The only qualification for a show jumper is that it should be able to jump; and there is no special type or breed of horse that jumps better than another. One only has to consider for a moment the completely different types that have been top-class show jumpers since the war.

Foxhunter was three-quarter bred, his sire being a thoroughbred. Sunsalve was the same, and it is probably true to say that the majority of good jumpers are thoroughbred, but few are out of thoroughbreds. Prince Hall, of course, was clean-bred, but Pat Smythe's other famous horse, Tosca, was of very humble origin, being bred out of a draft mare in Ireland. Craven A, reserve in our gold medal team in Helsinki and a prolific winner in the fifties for Peter Robeson, was out of a shire mare: as was the famous Nizefela on which Wilf White won an Olympic medal.

The diminutive Dundrum is part Connemara: little Stroller is only a pony, while Merely-a-Monarch is over 17 h.h.

Many good horses come from Ireland, and indeed it is on Irish-bred horses that the famous Italian brothers d'Inzeo have won many of the greatest prizes: but probably the German horses, particularly the mighty Hanoverians, are the most suitable of all for show jumping, because of their great strength and scope.

25

TYPE OF HORSE

From all of which it will be appreciated that top-class show jumpers come in all shapes and sizes. One cannot, therefore, set out with any specific picture in one's mind if one is going to buy a jumper.

What one can do, however, is to be clear about particular qualities in the conformation of a horse one is buying as a jumper. Not only must a horse be basically sound, but he must in certain respects have those qualities which one knows are going to help a horse whether he is large or small, fast or slow. It may be as well to consider these under different headings.

TEMPERAMENT

Because, when all is said and done, it is *accuracy* that is more essential than anything else if a horse is to jump consistently well, then obviously the better a horse's temperament the better a horse is likely to jump. If a horse is very erratic, very highly strung, very headstrong, it is obviously going to be much harder for the rider to steady him, balance him, 'place' him, with the result that his jumping will be inaccurate.

Admittedly there have been many outstanding jumpers of international standard that have possessed anything but easy temperaments: but they have needed outstanding riders to manage them.

A horse with an equable temperament, moreover, will take far less out of himself, which will not only result in his being easier to keep fit, but will enable him to remain fresh through to the final jump-off.

It is true, possibly, that a horse can have too good a temperament, so that he is in fact positively lazy: but for the less experienced there can be no doubt that it is easier to achieve success with a lazy horse, providing he has the jumping ability, than with a highly strung horse.

It must be remembered too that contrary to what one might expect, the more a horse jumps the keener he will get. It has been said that jumping is to a horse as alcohol is to a man. They

26

become increasingly excited and excitable which is why one so often sees a novice horse jumping in a plain snaffle at the beginning of a season, but by the end of the season having all manner of contraptions in his mouth. This, as will be explained later, can be avoided if the rider is patient enough, is prepared to take time and avoid the temptation to progress too quickly.

A final word about temperament. Although it is true that a horse like any other animal will inherit certain characteristics from its parents, it is equally true that his temperament will largely evolve from the person with whom he is associated. In other words if a groom or rider is nervous, excitable, impatient, these characteristics will quickly become apparent in the horse; whereas a groom or rider that is quiet and calm will almost invariably get a quiet and calm reaction from a horse.

How often one sees a horse have the last fence down in an otherwise clear round. This is because the excitement of the rider has communicated itself to the horse. In the same way it is the child's anxiety or apprehension that communicates itself to a pony when it refuses the first fence.

COLOUR

It is virtually true to say that colour plays very little part in the quality of a horse. There is a certain amount of justification for believing that a jet black horse is inclined to have a will of its own: that a bright chestnut mare is often rather hot and 'fussy': that a very pale chestnut horse may be lacking a little in courage.

There is no doubt that a horse with white socks is liable to have trouble with its heels—cracked heels and so on. A coloured horse, or skewbald or piebald, will seldom have sufficient scope for a jumper; though a coloured pony is seldom lacking in this respect. It is quite certain that bay or brown is a good hard colour, and most people who have been concerned with horses all their lives are of the opinion that horses of these colours are less likely to give trouble from the health point of view.

TYPE OF HORSE

But again there are so many contradictions to these 'theories' that it is unwise to pontificate on the subject. It is, too, not without interest that today there seems to be a noticeable increase in greys and chestnuts (greys as a rule are born as chestnuts) and correspondingly a decrease in the number of bays and browns bred.

THE SIZE

As has already been said, show jumpers come in all shapes and sizes, but just as the pony that can jump as big and as high as a horse is a freak, so, as a general rule, a very overgrown, clumsy horse is unlikely to be a good jumper. Admittedly its very size makes the fence appear small, but usually a horse that is unnaturally big lacks the necessary activity: especially in the sort of competition that ultimately depends on speed: and, of course, this is the case with the majority. Only in Puissance competitions (the show jumping equivalent of the high jump) does the clock not come into the reckoning, and few people can afford to keep a horse solely for Puissance competitions. There have been horses such as the mighty Meteor, ridden by Franz Theidemann of Germany, who virtually competed only in Puissance and Nations' Cups (team events over particularly big courses).

What is of definite importance, as far as size is concerned, is the scope of a horse. Whether large or small he should stand over a lot of ground: 'a leg at each corner' is one way of describing this. A horse must not have his feet close together, be too narrow or give the appearance of being much longer from wither to tail than from front feet to hind feet.

MOVEMENT

A jumper is not, of course, a show horse that has to excel in conformation, but it will obviously be to its advantage if its action is *straight*, if only because if it throws its feet about it

28

will be perpetually bruising itself as a hoof hits a joint. It is less troublesome if a horse moves wide behind rather than close behind. Similarly it is likely to cause trouble if a horse moves very close in front. At worst it can cross its legs and come down: at best it will hit itself.

High knee action, unsightly to those who like to see a fluent movement, is not necessarily a deterrent in a jumper. Often it denotes hackney blood in the veins, and many top-class jumpers have come from hackneys.

A horse that goes sideways as opposed to straight is generally a horse that has been badly broken, has been allowed to get into bad habits, or is temperamentaly difficult.

THE HEAD

Plenty of great jumpers have had big ugly heads: the shape of the head can in no way affect a horse's jumping ability, but the eye is of the utmost importance. A wild eye will inevitably betray a wild character. A big, honest eye, well set, with the minimum of white showing, will generally denote an honest, generous type of horse.

Although some people are suspicious of small ears, insisting that it suggests meanness, and others have strong feelings about small nostrils set rather close together, suggesting that this can lead to a respiratory trouble, it is, I think, of greater importance to be satisfied with the mouth. Parrot-mouth, with the upper teeth overlapping the lower, not only can lead to feeding difficulties but is often the cause of a bad mouth.

Obviously the telling of age by the teeth is important, but it is not wholly relevant here.

When buying a horse it is worth inspecting carefully the corners of the mouth. If they are scarred and sore it will almost certainly mean that the horse is a puller.

Like the head the shape of the neck is relatively unimportant. A scraggy ewe-neck is not very pretty and often it means that a horse is not as easy to mouth as it should be, but there have been

29

TYPE OF HORSE

many good horses with bad necks. More difficult, though perhaps less unattractive, is the horse with the bull neck which is invariably very strong, and therefore exhausting to ride.

A high head carriage is almost invariably a good quality. Not only is the horse's outlook improved, but it also means that the head and neck are properly set on to the horse's body. A horse with a low head carriage is always difficult to ride. His balance is wrong and, of course, he is hanging on one's hands all the time. It is more difficult to adjust his stride because the relationship between leg and hand is wrong.

THE FORELEG

A horse must have good limbs if it is going to stand up to the strain of jumping. Although a strong sloping shoulder is not so important as in the horse that is essentially needed to gallop or give a comfortable ride, nevertheless a well-sloped shoulder increases a horse's scope, and automatically shifts the weight of the rider back into the centre of the horse's back where it should be. If a horse is straight of shoulder then automatically the rider will be sitting up close to the withers which puts the whole balance wrong.

A horse can be over at the knee or back at the knee. The former is preferable, for the latter creates a severe strain on the tendons down the back of the canon bone.

Particularly important is the bone below the knee. This has to take the entire weight of the horse's body and the additional weight of the rider. It should be at least eight inches in circumference. Less bone can only lead to trouble. Too great a strain will be put on the supporting tendons, which is what leads to horses breaking down.

The joints and the fetlock should be clean, though it is likely that with age and work they will become somewhat rough and nobbly. In the same way the tendons will get puffy and windgalls will appear. But though these things are unsightly and need very careful attention if a horse is to keep sound it is not necessarily the end of a show jumper if the ideal cleanness of limbs and joints is not apparent.

The link between the fetlock joint and the foot is the pastern. This in fact is the spring without which a horse could never jump and scarcely move. If it is too straight or too short then there is not enough spring. If it is too sloping then there is again a strain on the tendons.

However good limbs horses may have they are useless unless they also have good feet. Veterinary surgeons will say that more unsoundness comes from the foot than any other part of the body: and much of it is due to man. In other words comparatively few horses are born with bad feet: occasionally one sees a horse with a confined, upright, boxy foot, instead of the proper sloping broad-based foot, but so often by not being properly cared for horses' feet are allowed to grow into the wrong shape, and this quickly leads to trouble. If they grow out in front then a horse will find itself forced on to its heels with the resultant strain again on the tendons. If they are badly shod the foot becomes pinched which will lead to navicular, for which there is really no cure. But shoeing too can lead to pricks and corns and other discomforts which will make it impossible for a horse to jump his best.

THE BODY

A horse that is too compact may lack scope: a horse that is too long may be weak across the loins and be liable to strain, though there have been good horses both too compact and too long. Much more important is the girth. Unless a horse has sufficient depth through the heart he will always be at a disadvantage in the operation of his lungs: and of his heart too. A good, deep rib cage allows a horse plenty of room for the working of the most important parts of his motor. For the same reason a horse does not want to be too narrow.

Admittedly a very deep horse can be somewhat short in the leg, or give the appearance of being too short in the leg: this would limit his scope but often this can be compensated for by the power and strength of the horse in the quarters. Mr. Robert Hanson's Olympic horse Flanagan is a good example of this.

In theory a horse 'on the leg' should be a better jumper, but this is not always so. A horse showing too much daylight between the ground and the undercarriage can lack strength, and frequently has not as much bone as he should have.

Substance must be of importance in a horse; as far as a show jumper is concerned, if one has to choose between quality and substance, then it is the latter that is the priority. Substance means strength, and strength is essential in a show jumper.

A racehorse has, firstly, to have stamina because a race can be anything between 5 furlongs and $4\frac{1}{2}$ miles. He also has to have speed. But for a show jumper it is quite different. No course is longer than 800 yards and therefore stamina scarcely comes into it: hence for a show jumper to be gone in the wind is not necessarily a handicap. Admittedly the final jump off is probably against the clock, but the winner is likely to be the one that can turn quickest rather than the one that can gallop fastest. Speed, therefore, is not all that important. What is important is strength. There may be as many as eighteen or twenty fences in that 800 yards: often they are only a few yards apart: often they involve sharp changes of direction. A weak or frail-framed horse could never stand up to it.

THE HIND LEG

All the motive power comes from behind the saddle. This is where the real strength must lie. Without any doubt the first essential in a show jumper is good quarters and good hocks. As with the foreleg the bone must be strong and clean, the pasterns resilient, the feet good, whereas no horse with weak quarters or bad hocks will ever make a jumper.

Often people will say that the highest part of a horse's quarters is his jumping bump, especially if it is particularly protuberant, but this is not an absolute fact. The important thing is that the

1. 'The next to jump . . .'. A rider enters the famous Horse of the Year Show arena at Wembley.

2. World Champion. Marion Coakes winner of the Ladies World Championship in 1965 on her brilliant 14·2 h.h. pony, Stroller.

quarters should be big, rounded and strong. A horse's finest muscles should be in his quarters: there should be ample length between the hip joint and the hindest part of the quarters. The quarters should be well built up thus giving the horse a high tail carriage. A horse with a low tail carriage is seldom a first-class horse, whereas for some not very apparent reason a horse that carries its tail high is usually a horse of courage and stamina. Even at the end of a race Arkle's high tail carriage is particularly noticeable.

The hock is an extremely delicate and complex joint, but its proper functioning is vital to the jumper. A weak hock will always give trouble. Hocks standing too far away from a horse rather than well under him will cause strain. Any suspicion of a curb—a bowing out of the tendon immediately below the joint —betrays a weakness which can only lead to trouble.

Cow hocks, when the joints turn in towards each other, are not only unsightly but will again lead to strain. Spavins and thoroughpins are unsoundnesses, and one is taking a risk in working such horses, though professional veterinary advice may result in a horse standing if it has been fired or blistered.

Between the quarters and the hock comes the second thigh. Many experts will insist that this vital link is more important than anything else. A narrow tapering second thigh will so often turn out to be the weak link. A good strong second thigh on the other hand will enable the power of the quarters and strength of the quarters to work in perfect co-ordination causing no undue strain anywhere in the hind leg.

To sum up: although there is no prototype of a show jumper yet there are certain qualities that will be found in good jumpers, and should be sought by those looking for a jumper.

Good bone, good feet, depth through the girth, and above all a strong hind leg: these are the absolutely essential ingredients in the hotch-potch of colours, shapes and sizes that make up show jumpers.

CHAPTER III

Types of Fences

As important as the fences themselves is the general design of the course. Over the years much research has been carried out as regards course building. Many years ago the course consisted of some ten fences, most of them gorse hurdles or white poles, set in a figure of eight.

Nowadays there will be as many as sixteen or eighteen different fences, and far from being gorse hurdles they will be everything from miniature viaducts to grass banks; far from being straight-forward poles they will be tubs filled in with flowering shrubs, pot plants, oil drums painted gaudy colours. Far from being a simple figure of eight the course will have endless 'changes of direction', one fence being set at right angles to another: the same fences even being jumped from each direction. There will be doubles and trebles, upright fences and spread-fences.

All this is, firstly, to provide a more interesting test for the horse and rider; and secondly to appear attractive to the spectator, for it must always be remembered that show jumping is basically a spectator sport.

In a human jumping competition the entire purpose is to find who can jump the highest. This is not so with show jumping: indeed in most countries the high jump has been abolished as it is felt that the strain is too great for a horse. It has been replaced by the 'Puissance', a competition in which there are only a very few big fences, but unlike the high jump when the horses go on jumping until the limit has been reached—and it should be remembered that it is only when the horse is tiring that the

34

greatest heights are attempted—in the puissance the competition is limited to four jumps-off.

A clever course designer—or a cunning one—could build a course in which no fence is higher than 4 ft. but over which no horse could go clear. The reason for this, of course, would be the way the fences were placed in relation to each other. In the Olympic Games at Wembley a water jump 16 ft. broad was followed only some eight or nine strides away by a 5 ft. 3 in. wall. A rider going fast enough to clear the water could not possibly steady his horse sufficiently in time to jump the wall, and so many riders purposely jumped into the water for 4 faults believing that to be preferable to crashing through the wall and possibly falling, for a total of 12 faults—4 for hitting the wall and 8 for falling.

In the same way at the Rome Olympics the water was followed by a set of parallel poles which were at right angles to the water. If one had sufficient speed to clear the water it was almost impossible to turn the corner in time to jump the poles.

These, of course, are extreme examples, but they illustrate the importance of the design of the course. A good designer is trying to produce a course which will find out the best horse and rider; and the good horse and rider will be capable of jumping a big, difficult, twisty course better than a bad horse and rider, because they will be jumping in a properly controlled manner.

Show jumping is not a race, and therefore a course should not be too straightforward. An inexperienced course builder will design a course that allows a horse to gallop round it flat out, with the minimum of control from the rider. With luck he may meet all the fences right and jump a clear round, but such a course gives no advantage to the better horse and rider. Today course builders and show organizers are always trying to provide a competition that will produce the most talented combination of horse and rider as the winner.

As a general rule a course designer will hope to build a course that will produce one clear round in every five. This will provide, say, six clear rounds. In some competitions, as explained in the next chapter, the fences will be raised for the first jump-off, but it will not be against the clock. This should produce three for a final jump-off, which is against the clock. It is here that skill and experience really count, as to jump big fences in a twisty course at speed is a real test. It is in this way that the best horses come out on top. Often enough a careless mistake, or bad luck, will eliminate a top-class horse before the final jump-off: but it is extremely unlikely that a bad or inexperienced horse will finish up the winner.

From the above it will be appreciated that to make show jumping interesting and attractive both to the rider and to the spectator the course must have plenty of variety. This variety is achieved firstly by the actual elements used in building the fences—today they can be full of originality, such as chicken coups, level crossing gates or wheelbarrows—and secondly by the way these elements are used.

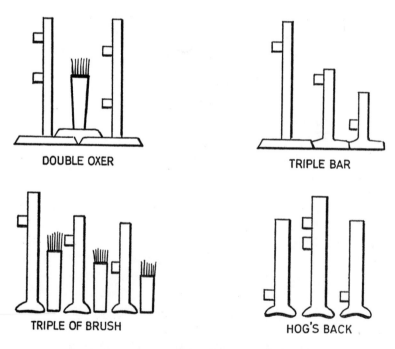

DOUBLE OXER

TRIPLE BAR

TRIPLE OF BRUSH

HOG'S BACK

FIG. A. *Side view of different spread fences*

36

TYPES OF FENCES

There are really three kinds of fences: the straight fence, the spread fence and the combination, which consists of two or three fences all close enough together to be regarded by the rider and the horse as a single problem.

It is the careful mixing of these fences that is the coursebuilder's job. A course entirely of uprights would be dull indeed —though such courses are occasionally introduced such as the six bars competition (see next chapter). A course consisting entirely of spread fences would be too exhausting for the horse as obviously there is an additional strain if a horse has to achieve width as well as height. Occasionally there is a course consisting entirely of combinations, but this is something of a gimmick and only introduced at big shows lasting as much as a week, when a course designer is hard up to it to think up sufficient variations of competitions.

THE STRAIGHT FENCE

The straight upright fence more or less explains itself. All its elements are placed vertically to the ground, one above the other. There must be nothing either in front of it or behind it: no ground rail or ditch.

The simplest example of a straight fence is a gate or a single pole. The average-sized gate is 4 ft.—but, of course, by lifting it off the ground it can be considerably higher. Gates need not always be white or five-bar. Frequently rustic gates are used, or fancy gates such as the famous Helsinki gate named after a fence built for the Helsinki Olympics when an ornamental gate with a concave top (the middle lower than the sides) was hung between two high uprights.

A simple pole is an extremely difficult fence to jump because, having nothing underneath it, it lacks a ground-line. When approaching a fence, a horse will always judge the point of take-off by looking at the line of the base of the fence: this is called the ground line. If there are several poles beneath the top pole it will be easier for the horse to see the ground line and, of

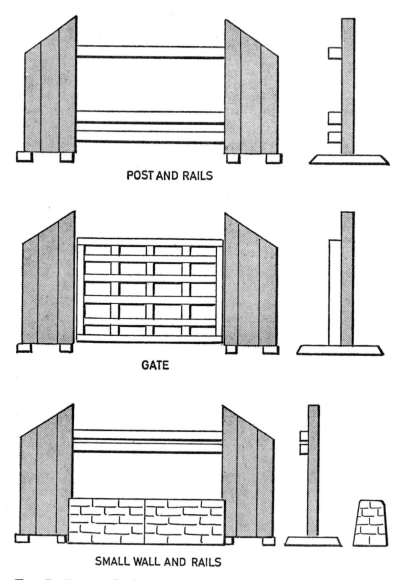

POST AND RAILS

GATE

SMALL WALL AND RAILS

FIG. B. *Front and side views upright fence, gate and small spread, wall in front of poles*

course, if there is a pole actually lying on the ground it will be easier still.

A wall is generally a straight fence, though if a pole or a box of flowers or shrubs is placed in front of it it becomes a spread fence. Occasionally, such as at Dublin and Lucerne, there is a solid stone wall which is a permanent part of the show ground,

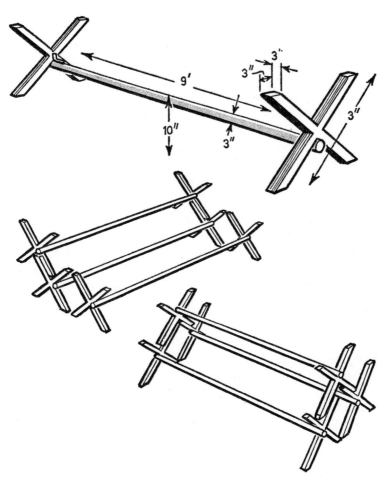

FIG. C. *Cavaletti, showing how simple arrangement of them makes them into a simple fence*

but more usually the wall is artificial, built in sections of wood: fir boarding, planed, is as effective as anything. The bricks that make the top are also of wood. Though the wall, therefore, has a very solid appearance, which will encourage a horse to jump it well, it will in fact be comparatively light and fall easily, causing a horse no damage whatever, though giving a considerable amount of trouble to the arena party who have to rebuild it!

As a rule a simple upright brush fence is used as the first fence in a course. This just enables a horse to get warmed up and, as it were, into his stride before he encounters the bigger obstacles. A course builder is not trying to catch a horse out and therefore he is as anxious as the rider himself that the horse should get safely over the two or three easy fences at the beginning of a course.

THE SPREAD FENCE

As the name suggests the spread fence has width as well as height. The obvious example is the water jump. A water jump has to be included in an international team event—a Nations' Cup—and it must be at least 10 ft. wide to be called a water jump. An Olympic water jump is 15 or even 16 ft. The fence in front of it is never more than 2 ft. 6 in. high and as a rule is built so that it slopes towards the water which encourages the horse to spread. It is, in fact, similar to the water jump in a steeplechase.

But water can be used in other ways: before or after a fence, underneath a fence, or entirely on its own. All these are variations of the spread fence.

Another obvious spread fence is the triple bar: it is more common than any other spread fence used in this country, many shows not having water jumps. Although it is an impressive-looking fence it is easy to jump because it is so inviting to the horse, the poles being graded towards the top. The front rail should be quite low—18 in. or 2 ft.: the distance between the final and second rail should be the same as the distance between the second and third rail. The difference in height between the first and second rail should be slightly greater than the distance in height between the second and third rail.

As it is an inviting fence the spread should not be less than the height of the last, the highest pole. If the height of the fence is 4 ft. 6 in. the spread could be 4 ft. 6 in. or 5 ft. If the height is 5 ft. the spread could be as much as 6 ft.

A variation of the triple is the hog's back. This is identical to the triple except that the last pole instead of being higher than the second is lower, normally the same height as the first pole.

Both the triple bar and the hog's back have, as a rule, a brush or some sort of fill-in below the first pole, if it is more than 18 in. off the ground. With an oxer, however, this is not the case and in consequence it is a far more difficult fence. The oxer stands in front of a brush fence, the distance between the two being something like 2 ft.: but the oxer itself is 3 ft. high so that it has no ground line. The horse in fact is looking at the bottom of the brush fence for its ground line, and will therefore tend to take off too close to the fence not realizing that the pole is 2 ft. nearer to him than the fence.

In the case of a double oxer another pole the same height and distance from the fence stands out on the landing side. As the horse cannot see it until he has taken off there is a likelihood of his jumping short and hitting the pole. The oxer is based on the fences most likely to be met out hunting in the Midlands before barbed wire had been invented.

The most difficult of spread fences is the parallel poles. They may be as much as 7ft. 6 in. apart in a really high-class competition, and as high as 5 ft. or higher, but having no ground line under either of the poles they make an extremely difficult obstacle. The fence will be slightly easier if the first pole is fractionally lower than the second pole: but if the poles are a true parallel then it is a very difficult fence indeed. By putting shrubs or any kind of fill-in under the poles it will make it less difficult, though the difficulty of this particular fence lies as

41

much in the fact that the poles are the same height as in the fact that there is no ground line.

Obviously a ditch either in front or behind a fence will automatically turn it into a spread fence, but such ditches should not exceed 6 ft.

COMBINATIONS

If two, three or more fences are so placed that they closely follow one another with not more than 39 ft. 4 in. between any two (this apparently strange distance is the equivalent of 12 metres) then they constitute a combination and are judged as one fence. It is probably true to say that it is with a combination that the skill of horse and rider is most effectively tested.

The distance between the elements of the combination varies. It is decided by the number of strides the course builder expects a horse to take between two elements and the height and nature of the fences.

The average length of a horse's stride at full canter is 9 ft.: if for some reason, due to a sharp turn for instance, he is going slower, then the stride could only be 8 ft.: if he is really galloping on it could be 10 ft.

All this must be taken into consideration by the course builder as upon the pace of the horse's approach depends the distance between the elements of the combination.

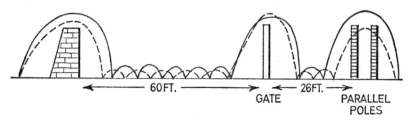

FIG. D. *Diagram showing how different length of stride can effect approach to fence. Firm line is correct: dotted line shows how landing too short over wall means loss of impulsion for double*

TYPES OF FENCES

As a general rule the distance between two fences, if the horse is expected to take two strides, will be 24 ft. This distance is arrived at as follows: a horse will land 4 ft. away from the average-sized fence: each stride will be 8 ft.: the horse will take off 4 ft. from the second fence: total 24 ft. If a horse lands more than 4 ft. from the first fence then he will have to adjust the length of his strides in between, in particular the second stride which has been described as the hock-gathering stride.

The higher the fences the greater the distance needed between as the horse will land out further from the first fence and take off further from the second fence.

If the horse is expected to take three strides between the two elements of the combination, then the distance between will be approximately 35 ft. The distance between being greater it can be assumed that the horse will be going faster and therefore his stride will be 9 ft. or more, rather than 8 ft.

A one-stride combination will require about 16 ft. between the two fences: a stride of 8 ft. with 4 ft. for landing and 4 ft. for taking off.

It is interesting to realize that in theory a horse jumping a fence describes a perfect arc. The distance of take-off to the bottom of the fence is the same as the distance from the bottom of the fence to the point of landing, which in turn is equal to the height from the bottom of the fence to the highest point of the horse's jump.

In a treble (as opposed to a triple) when there are three elements in a combination, then the distance between will vary slightly according to the types of fences employed. If the second fence is higher than the first then the horse will land further out over it than over the first and the distance between the second and the third will have to be greater. If in addition the third fence is higher than the second then the distance will have to be greater still as the horse will be standing back further for his take-off.

If the second or third element in a combination is a spread fence as opposed to an upright then the distance in front of it will have to be reduced, otherwise the horse will have to reach for the fence and will probably fail to make the spread.

43

TYPES OF FENCES

To encourage novice horses to jump combinations well it is essential that the distances should be correct, but in top-class competitions if the distances are occasionally slightly incorrect then it will make the rider use his intelligence in deciding just how he should cope with the problem posed. Does he want to approach fast and land well out over the first element so that he can reach the second in two strides? or will he do better to approach slowly, landing close to the first element, and then easily fitting in three strides before the second element? But if he decides on the latter will he then have sufficient impulsion to reach the third element in two strides? Or if he has to do it in three will he be able to stand off far enough for the third element to clear the first of the parallel poles.

A single example will suffice to show the problems with which a rider is faced in deciding how to tackle a combination where the distances are incorrect, and at the same time show how dangerous it can be if intentionally or unintentionally the course builder sets a trap.

At the Rome Olympic Games there was a treble, the first element of which was an upright wall: the second and third elements were spreads—a triple bar and parallel poles: the distance between the first two elements was 23 ft. 9 in. and the distance between the second two was 29 ft. 6 in.

Twenty-nine ft. six in. This obviously presented a problem. Should one take one or two strides between the triple and the parallels; 29 ft. 6 in. was almost equidistant between the 24 ft. normal for one stride and 36 ft. normal for two. (Apparently for no reason that has ever been explained the International Federation Technical Delegate had insisted on this last distance being altered by 6 ft., thus turning it into a trap).

By the time David Broome on Sunsalve entered the arena, the sixteenth to jump, no single rider had cleared the treble: a number had had falls. All had tried to fit in three strides in that 29 ft. 6 in., had failed, and crashed through the parallels. David Broome, however, knowing the immense scope of Sunsalve had decided to approach very fast and put in only two strides.

TYPES OF FENCES

It nearly came off, but not quite. Sunsalve just failed to reach the second of the parallel poles. But it was a near miss.

Much to everyone's surprise in the second round he decided on the same course, though it appeared to the spectator as though he had shown that even Sunsalve could not do it in two strides. In fact David Broome had realized that Sunsalve's failure to reach the parallels in the first round was not in any way due to lack of scope, but was because turning the corner to approach the treble he suddenly hesitated, confronted with the brilliant reflection of the newly-painted red wall which had the early morning sun full on it. As a result he lost vital impulsion without which he could not make the third element.

At his second attempt, ridden with superb confidence by David Broome, he literally sailed through and indeed succeeded in making it look easy. He was in fact the only horse to take two strides between the triple and the parallels, and almost the only horse to clear it at all.

This anecdote will show how experienced a rider must be in planning the way he is to ride a course. It also shows the unfortunate troubles than can be caused if unwittingly a builder sets a trap. It also shows both the opportunities open to, and the experience needed by, a course builder in planning a course, combining all the different obstacles and types of obstacles at his disposal.

CHAPTER IV

Types of Courses

As already stated show jumping is not just a matter of who can jump highest. It is a test of skill both of horse and rider. Nor is it an exclusive sport: rather it is a spectator sport.

It is for this reason that the courses are varied. A course designer is seeking to test horses in different ways, and according to what he is looking for so he plans his courses.

Basically it is true to say that there are two types of courses: those where time is all important, and those where it is less so. Today the majority of competitions have a final jump-off against the clock, when the horse with the fastest time is the winner. But this is only a last resort, as it were. When two or more horses are still undivided after one or more jumps-off, then rather than go on indefinitely raising the jumps to dangerous heights and exhausting the horses time is introduced. In addition this prevents a competition from becoming boring to the spectators. Indeed it does the opposite, for nothing is more exciting than a good jump-off against the clock.

The advantage of a speed competition from the point of view of the show organization is that one can assess exactly how long such a competition will last, as there is, except on very rare occasions, no need for a jump-off, the winner being the rider with the fastest time in the first round.

For this reason it is usually the practice at a big show to start with a speed event, the organizers knowing exactly how much time to allow for the event. In an ordinary competition it is always possible to make a mistake in the number of clear rounds allowed for, and therefore a competition timed to last 75 minutes might last over $1\frac{1}{2}$ hours, thus throwing the whole time-table out for the rest of the performance.

Or, of course, it can happen the other way—less clear rounds than expected meaning that the competition finishes early, again throwing out the programme.

It does not matter so much if a competition overruns or underruns at the end of the programme, as no other class is being interfered with.

There are many different kinds of speed events, all of which provide interest and variety for those who take part and those who watch. It is almost true to say that the speed event was introduced into show jumping to add to a programme a little light relief: but more than that it provides a rider with the opportunity to jump successfully a horse that will never make the heights associated with the big jumping competitions.

Most riders have two types of horse, the one that is capable of jumping a big course in which time is comparatively unimportant, and the other that is capable of coping with a speed course.

As a rule the fences are never higher than 4 ft. 6 in. in a speed competition, and a course builder will always be very careful to make sure that he is building nothing that could be dangerous when jumped at speed.

He will, of course, make the course tricky, full of twists and turns, thus testing the agility of the horse and the control that the rider has of it. Every extra yard can take an extra second. On the other hand, trying to turn a horse too sharp can result in a horse losing its impulsion, and thus reducing its speed. It can also lead to its not having enough speed and impulsion to jump the next fence.

Speed competitions under international rules are jumped under Table B or Table C. These are slight variations in the methods of judging. For instance one can have a straightforward speed event when the lowest score with the fastest time is the winner; or one can have an event when each fence knocked down adds so many seconds to the time. If, say, a horse takes 45 seconds but has two fences down then, if the penalty is 5 seconds per fence, his final score will be 55 seconds.

Then there is the Touch and Out competition. In this a horse is allowed to jump for a specified time, say 1 minute, and can jump as many fences as he possibly can in that time—until he hits one, then he has to retire. If he completes the course then he starts again and goes on jumping until his minute is up. If the bell rings before he has actually landed over a fence then that fence does not count.

There are various kinds of Relay races that can be included in a programme as a speed event. There is the sraightforward relay, one rider handing the baton to the next, their two scores being added together: or there is the Rescue Relay when if the first rider makes a mistake, the second rider has to take over, carrying on until he makes a mistake when the first rider takes over again. This competition, as can be imagined, can be highly amusing, especially if riders make mistakes at consecutive fences.

The Take Your Own Line Competition is frequently put on as a speed event. Competitors can jump the fences in any order that they like within a specified time. With ingenuity a course designer can build a course with endless alternative routes so that no two riders will choose the same way round, each rider believing his way to be the quickest: and, of course, the safest. The really skilled rider and experienced horse will take the risk of jumping a really big fence from just a few strides of approach and get away with it. Another will try it and fail.

As a rule, in a Take Your Own Line the fences are built so that they can be jumped in either direction, and generally there is a rule that no fence may be jumped more than once.

Watching riders walk the course before a Take Your Own Line one sees them pondering and pausing and trying to memorize as they work out the best route.

Have-a-gamble is another form of speed event. In this competition there is a course of fences varying very much in size. The smaller fences are not worth very much, but the bigger fences are worth much more. Often the scoring is done through the

3. Olympic medallist. Peter Robeson on Firecrest on which he won the bronze medal at Tokyo in 1964. He was reserve at Helsinki in 1952 and team bronze medallist at Stockholm in 1956.

4a & b. European Champions. David Broome European Champion on Mister Softie in 1967, and on Sunsalve (*below*) in 1962.

medium of playing cards, large facsimiles of which are attached to each fence. A rider jumping the Ace will get perhaps a hundred, a King is worth 90, a Queen 80, a Knave 70, while the lower cards are only worth 40. Generally each fence can be jumped twice and sometimes three times: but if a fence is once knocked down it cannot be jumped again. The winner is the rider with the highest score within a specified time.

In speed events competitors are not penalized for a refusal, other than adding inevitably to the time taken.

Although a certain number of straight or upright obstacles will be included in a speed course to test the control and collection of horse and rider, the whole object of the event is to encourage horses to go fast. The majority of fences therefore should be of an inviting nature and comparatively easy.

The course should be tricky but never trappy. Frequently a rider will introduce a horse to top-class jumping by entering it in a speed event: or a rider will use a speed event to restore the confidence of a horse that has lost its nerve over the bigger fences. It is an ideal way of sharpening up a horse if it has become a little sluggish. The last thing one wants, therefore, is an accident, a bad fall which could well destroy a horse's confidence.

Speed events have a great appeal to the crowd for from the very first horse tension is considerable, as one rider tries to improve upon the fastest time so far.

But although big shows always include speed events, offer good prize money for them and attract top-class horses, it is the straightforward competitions jumped under Table A of the international rules that are the really important ones.

These major events always have a time allowance and a time limit, and usually have a jump-off against the clock, but they are in no sense speed events. The course designer is doing something totally different when he builds a course for straightforward jumping competitions. He is firstly testing the scope of a horse, by building fences that are high or wide or both. Secondly, he is testing the balance of the horse in that by the position of the fences in relation one with another he will discover which horses can change direction and be sufficiently balanced to jump a big fence a few strides away. Thirdly, by introducing changes of direction he is ensuring that the rider is sufficiently controlled. Finally he is testing the courage of a horse, for a bold horse is needed to jump big fences, and, in combinations particularly, if a horse hesitates he must inevitably lose his impulsion and fail to make the end of the jump.

In the average open jumping competition the fences vary from 4 ft. 6 in. to 5 ft. 3 in. with spreads from 4 ft. to 7 ft. Occasionally in big competitions the fences are bigger, and naturally in a jump-off they will go considerably higher than the original. But a good course builder will always see that the fences are safe. Obviously it is possible at any fence for a horse to get in a muddle for one reason or another, make a mistake and come down, perhaps injuring itself. But this is not necessarily the fault of the course builder.

In an open jumping competition there are always combinations included, at least one double and one treble and possibly more. The course as a rule is almost 800 yds long and the speed is estimated at approximately 350 yds to the minute. This means that if the course was 700 yds. long the time allowance would be 2 minutes. Any competitor taking longer would be penalized (see later chapter). The time limit is always twice the time allowance. In a 700-yard course, therefore, it would be 4 minutes. If a competitor takes longer than this then he would be eliminated.

Just as there are variations in a speed event so there are variations of a straightforward event: but there are not so many of them.

The more usual are the Accumulator, the Six Bars and the Puissance.

In the former there are only five or seven obstacles, but they are progressively difficult. The first fence, the easiest, wins the competitor one point, the second fence two points and so on, until the last fence which, if cleared, adds seven points to the competitor's score. A maximum score, therefore, is 28.

TYPES OF COURSES

The Six Bars is a competition jumped over a line of six posts and rails and can be extremely spectacular. The poles are placed at distances apart of 35 ft. The distances between the last two and the penultimate two being perhaps a little greater as the poles get higher.

Although some course builders have all the poles at the same height it is more usual to have them progressively higher starting a little below 4 ft. and rising to 5 ft. 3 in. or even 5 ft. 6 in. After the first jump-off the six poles are reduced to four as they are raised, and for the final jump-off they are reduced to three.

The poles go up 4 in. each round and as can be imagined with only three strides between each pole this is an extremely testing competition.

The Six Bars has a certain similarity with the Puissance or 'Test' Competition. In this event there are only some seven fences but they are all big. The time allowance is generous, almost 300 yards to the minute, so time does not really come into it.

All those who jump clear rounds jump again, but only over five fences, which are raised. The next and subsequent jumps-off are over only two fences, usually a big spread of parallel poles, or a triple bar, and an upright wall. By now the fences may well be over 6 ft. Eventually they can stand at 7 ft. or more.

This competition has replaced the old High Jump Competition which is not regarded with favour in international circles nowadays as it is felt that it is only when the horse is getting tired that he is asked to jump the really big heights. The Puissance on the other hand is more like a straightforward competition, but over fewer fences and with no jump-off against the clock.

Finally, there are the team events. If they are international they are known as Nations' Cups. As a rule it is a long course and a testing one, the heights varying from 4 ft. 3 in. to 5 ft. 3 in. Combinations should be included, and a water jump. How often has Britain lost a Nations' Cup through one or more of its team faulting at the water—a prevalent British fault!

The greatest of all Team Event courses, is, of course, the

51

Olympic Games which will be dealt with in a later chapter. Although a course builder must remember that he is constructing a course for a team and therefore all the horses competing may not be top-class horses, it would be a mistake to build an unduly small course. The object of a Team Event is to find out the best team, and the best team is the team that has the most top-class horses.

Occasionally there can be a tie in a team event, when, as in an ordinary Competition, there is a jump-off: but in this case it is the whole team that jumps-off, each competitor being timed so that in the event of further equality the aggregate time of the whole team would count and the fastest team be the winner.

Although such as Foxhunter Competitions and Area International Trials are not in a special or different category, it may be worth writing of them briefly.

The Foxhunter competition was introduced to encourage novice horses to come into jumping. It was, of course, named after Col. Harry Llewellyn's famous horse and has been a success from the very start, introducing new horses into jumping many of which have become top class.

In Foxhunter Competitions no horse may have won more than £40. The course is a small one. The first three fences are limited to 3 ft. 6 in. Even in the final jump-off the fences must not exceed 4 ft. 3 in.

These Foxhunters are immensely popular and attract huge entries. Often they have to be jumped in two sections, and because of the number of entries they really need a ring to themselves at a show as the competition takes so long.

The whole competition is run in a series of local competitions culminating in a regional final. The winners of the regional final all go through to the grand final at the Horse of the Year Show at Wembley in October.

The Area International Trials are confined to Grade A horses and are designed to give selectors an opportunity of finding horses likely to make international horses. The courses, therefore, are expected to be solid and impressive. The course *must* include a water jump, and the competition should resemble in every respect an international event.

Unfortunately the Area International Trial has not been an unqualified success. Course builders do not always remember the international element, and show organizers tend to treat it as a poor relation. The reason for this is it is generally one of two big jumping competitions at a big show, the other being an ordinary Open which has probably been handsomely and generously subsidised by a sponsor, and therefore understandably given pride of place in the programme.

This is a pity because the Area International Trial should be channelling top-class horses into international levels just as the Foxhunters channel horses into top-class jumping.

Once again we find that variety is the key note with jumping. We have seen that every variety of horse is used: we have seen how varied the actual obstacles can be. Now we have seen how varied are the competitions themselves.

This is what makes jumping so interesting. A programme need never be dull. Not only can the variety of the horses, and even riders, taking part be of constant interest to the spectator; not only can the variety of obstacles provide a constantly interesting background to the jumping, but also the variety of the competitions can all the time present, for the interest of the spectator and for the skill of the rider, different problems demanding different methods, different tactics, different techniques.

A good show organizer will see that his programme is always well balanced. Speed events will alternate with big straightforward jumping competitions. There will be events for juniors, Foxhunters, team events, Area International Trials. There will be classes for Novices, special competitions for Lady riders. By thus varying the programme horses need never be overjumped, neither horse nor rider need get stale, spectators need never be bored. Once again variety has proved all important.

CHAPTER V

Early Training (I)

Most of those who have proved successful in show jumping, not only in Britain, but all over the world, have appreciated the fact that the basic training for any equestrian activity is what is known as schooling on the ground. In other words a horse must learn to walk before he can run. For a jumper this means that he must learn to carry himself, properly balanced, supple, and able to move correctly at each of the paces.

This, in fact, is nothing more nor less than what is today referred to as dressage. Unfortunately the use of this word, derived from the French, has frequently given rise to misunderstandings, with the result that in certain circles it is tantamount to a dirty word, people thinking that it only refers to high school riding, haute école, implying such complex and advanced movements as *piaffé, pirouette, passage.*

Nothing could be further from the truth. Many years ago Col. V. D. S. Williams, who was perhaps the real pioneer of dressage in this country when he first championed its values in the thirties, put it quite simply.

Dressage, he said, will benefit every riding horse required for field work, whether it be hunting, show jumping, combined training, hacking, polo, or even, to a certain degree, racing. This work, with a little assistance from an expert, can be practised successfully by any reasonably good horseman. It is, in reality, nothing more than the training taught in military schools of the past and employed in the training of cavalry mounts. A little more attention is, perhaps, paid to the accurate position of the

54

horse's head and body to ensure a more correct use of the impulsion muscles, so much needed in jumping. Furthermore the same methods have been employed subconsciously, to a certain extent, by many of the best natural horsemen in this country, the only difference being that it is now all included under the name of dressage. If any good horseman, who had not studied equitation, was asked how he made his horse perform any particular movement, he would most likely be at a loss to describe how it was done. One of the objects of dressage is to be able to explain and teach the methods employed by the experts, and learnt from many years of practice.

There is nothing new in dressage. That great French horseman, La Guérinière, who lived over two hundred years ago and on whose doctrines all the leading riding schools of Europe, including the Spanish Riding School and the French School at Saumur, base the main principles of their instruction, says in the first chapter of the book: 'The aim of training the horse is to make him quiet, supple and obedient by systematic work so that he becomes pleasant in his movements and comfortable for his rider. This applies in exactly the same way to the hunter, the charger or the school horse'—or the jumper.

First, then, it must be stressed how important a course of systematic field dressage is for the jumper. It develops the horse physically and mentally and prevents undue strain being put on the muscles and sinews before they are ready. By the correct and gradual development of these muscles, the risk of their being overstrained and of the horse being prematurely 'broken down' is greatly reduced, and the length of his useful life accordingly increased. By only asking the horse the very simplest of these exercises in the beginning and gradually leading on to more difficult ones, neither his intelligence nor his physical strength is overtaxed. He is kept mentally calm, becomes accustomed to authority and develops the habit of instant obedience.

Today the standard of jumping is high, and this field-dressage training for the jumper is absolutely essential. The horse is tested over long courses with frequent changes of direction. The horse must be as physically fit, as with muscles developed to the perfection of, any great athlete; further, if he is going to succeed, he must be absolutely obedient. Should he be subjected to competing in these competitions before he is fully trained, he may develop bad faults and break down.

I believe the improvement in the standard of our jumping in this country may be attributed to the study by our leading riders of this early training.

The very earliest training should be carried out on the lunge. Indeed many experts continue this method of training right through a jumper's education.

The following is the method most usually practised.

Put on a simple jointed snaffle and a saddle with the irons up. Fix the reins to the saddle in such a way that they do not interfere with the horse's mouth. The best type of noseband to use is a dropped noseband, which should be fitted below the bit so that the front strap is at least three fingers' width above the nostrils and the back lies in the chin groove. It should be so adjusted that when the horse's mouth is closed and steady he does not feel it, but it should be sufficiently tight to prevent him opening his mouth wide or crossing his jaw. Although a dropped noseband will not necessarily cure a horse that has contracted the habit of getting his tongue over the bit, it will almost certainly prevent him from starting the habit.

A cavesson, with a metal ring on the front of the noseband, should be placed over the top of the bridle. A lunge rein made of webbing, about 23 feet long, is then attached to the ring on the cavesson, never to the rings of the snaffle. Side-reins fixed to the girth, or to a proper lunging surcingle made to go over the saddle, are then fastened to the rings of the snaffle. These side-reins must be of equal length on both sides and must be adjusted so that, with a young horse, he can just reach them when his head is in the right position. On no account must they be too tight. They can be gradually shortened up as the horse improves in his training.

The lunge rein should be coiled in loops in such a way that they come easily off the hand as required. The rein is held in the hand to which the horse is being lunged, and the other hand carries a long whip—long enough for the lash to reach the horse but rarely to be used on him. It should be looked upon more as a directing pole, and the horse should have complete confidence in it.

If the horse is not accustomed to being lunged, the first few lessons must be devoted to getting him to go round the trainer in a circle. Once this has been accomplished, the horse must go at the pace required and he must obey implicitly all commands: this is most important for the future training.

In order to prevent the horse contracting the bad habit of dashing off at a fast pace, it is advisable always to commence the lesson at a walk. When this has been established, the horse is sent on at a good brisk trot, which is the pace at which most of the work on the lunge should be performed. The horse must always go out to the length of the lunge allowed him and, with a light but constant contact with it, must maintain a steady and well-cadenced pace. He should go equally well to either hand and must walk, trot, canter or halt at his trainer's command. At the halt he must remain out on the circle and only come in when called.

The trainer should not move about but remain on the same spot in the centre of the circle, except when moving the horse up to and over an obstacle.

JUMPING ON THE LUNGE

During this work on the lunge, the horse should be introduced to jumping, as this is an essential part of his training, whether it be intended that he should ultimately be a jumper or a hack; further it breaks the monotony of the training of the horse.

Before starting, the side-reins must always be removed. He should first be lunged over bars on the ground. These bars can later be exchanged for small jumps in the shape of parallel bars, walls, a brush fence or a miniature gate. Every new fence must be started practically on the ground and gradually raised as the horse takes it absolutely calmly. All this work must be done at the trot. If the horse shows any sign of excitement it is a sure indication that the fences are too high and they must be immediately lowered, if necessary until they are on the ground again. The jumping must be practised on both reins, and at this stage restraint must be exercised on the part of the trainer, as no matter how well the horse jumps, the fences must not be raised above 2 ft. 6 in. During this period these exercises should not be looked upon as jumping practice but more as suppling and obedience exercises to accustom the horse to jumping little fences with no sign of excitement.

A light pole fixed by a hook into a staple in the top of the upright of the jump should be used as a guide for the lunge-rein to slide over. Any disturbance or interference with the horse's head will destroy the smoothness of the jump.

MOUNTING

The next priority is mounting and how much inconvenience would be saved if this simple exercise in obedience was properly taught at the onset.

The horse must be taught to stand still to be mounted. This is the first and most important lesson in obedience. It can easily be obtained with a little patience. One stage should be practised at a time, and the next not proceeded with until the first is established. The rider should put his foot on the stirrup and take it out again and continue to do this until the horse stands. Next he puts some weight on the stirrup, and takes the foot out again if he moves, then he stands up in the stirrup and waits until the horse stands steady before finally throwing the leg over the saddle. Until the standstill is thoroughly confirmed it is a good thing for the rider to mount and dismount several times before moving off. The same remarks apply to dismounting; the rider must not do this until the horse not only stands still but stands squarely with his weight evenly distributed over all four legs.

EARLY TRAINING (I)

THE PACES:

THE WALK

The horse must not be allowed to move off into a walk unless he is standing correctly and until he gets the order from the rider. Great care must be taken to see that the horse remains on the bit and does not throw his head up when he moves off. If he does so, he must be brought back to the halt and made to repeat the movement until it is correctly executed. As soon as it is, he should be given his head and made to walk forward with a long swinging stride and with practically no contact with the reins. It is always advisable to do a good steady walk on a loose rein at the commencment of every lesson. Never try any collected work at the walk in the early stages of training; it shortens the horse's stride and is inclined to get him behind the bit.

A horse is said to be on the bit when he accepts the bit with his head in the right position and his hind legs under him. The whole object of dressage is to teach the horse to make the best use of his muscles for carrying his rider. By dressage one endeavours to get the horse's hind legs under him and to round his back by the subsequent lowering of the haunches. The moment he gets his head up above the natural position he hollows his back, sending his legs out behind him and making it more difficult for him to carry the weight. For this reason, every effort is made to prevent the horse from carrying the head too high, and to make him bring his hind legs under him, thus developing the muscles on his back and on the top of his neck. The easier the horse carries his rider, the easier and more fluent will be his action, and the prouder and happier will be his bearing: and the easier it will be for him to jump.

THE TROT

Keeping the horse on the bit plays the most important part in training, and great care must be taken to see that he stays on it during the transition from walk to trot. He must not throw his

59

head up; if he does, he must be brought back to a walk and made to move off again into a trot until he does it correctly.

When the horse is walking on a loose rein, take up the reins, get him on the bit and squeeze him forward with the legs into a trot. If he does not answer readily to the leg, tap him with a light swishy stick just behind the rider's leg or make use of the voice as was done when lunging. A click of the tongue will also be found very helpful in the early stages of training to keep the horse up to the bit and maintain the rhythm. Whip and voice must be abolished as training advances, and the horse must respond to the lightest pressure of the leg. The horse must be sent on at a good lively pace, and there must be the lightest contact with the mouth commensurate with keeping him on the bit.

Every horse is stiffer on one side than the other. If the horse gets his head up and pokes his nose, i.e. gets 'above the bit', the rider, whilst maintaining a steady contact with the soft side, should try to obtain a flexion on the hard or stiff side. This should not be attempted by a backward tension on the rein but by a squeezing and relaxing action of the hand, similar to that in squeezing a sponge. Every time this flexion is asked it must be accompanied by the use of the legs, the aid on the stiff side being the stronger. As soon as the horse gives, and comes down on the bit, relax and keep the hands as soft and quiet as possible. If an attempt is made to get the horse on the bit by a direct flexion, that is with an equal pressure on both reins, there is a danger of getting him overbent and shortening the stride. If difficulty is experienced, ride him in a large circle to the side to which he is stiff and, without losing contact with the outside rein, keep on trying to get a flexion to the inside. Every time this flexion is asked the rider must support it by a stronger pressure of the leg on the same side.

If the horse gets his head down too low, he must be pushed forward to get his hocks more under him. At this stage, it is no fault for the horse to reach forward and feel for the bit, as long as he does not lie on it or bring the angle of the face behind the perpendicular.

The horse must be sent on at a good active trot, but never

faster than he can manage, otherwise he will start quickening
and shortening his stride (running) instead of lengthening it. As
the training proceeds, and the horse's hocks get more under
him, it will be found that the length of the stride can be increased.

When the horse goes round the school and on a large circle,
at a good level pace, whilst maintaining contact with the bit by
a light feeling on the reins, changes of direction and serpentines
may be practised. A good exercise is from the wall to the wall.
On entering the long side of the school bring the horse away
from the track towards the centre of the school and then back
again to the track. At first only make the loop about a yard in
depth and gradually increase the size until it reaches the whole
way across the school. In all changes of direction, and in the
serpentines, great care must be taken to maintain the same
tempo and keep the horse on the bit.

THE CANTER

The canter should be attempted first from the trot, either on a
circle or when coming out of the corner at the short end of the
school. The rider's outside leg should be well drawn back, so
that a distinct difference is made between the aid for the canter
and the trot, and the horse urged into the canter by a stronger
pressure of both legs and a strong drive from the seat, the rider's
weight being slightly to the inside. As in the early lessons at the
trot, these aids may be reinforced by the whip and voice to
commence with. If the horse does not strike off on the required
leg, bring him back to a trot and immediately strike off again.

If the lunging has been correctly done, the rider should find
little difficulty in obtaining a true canter on either leg. During
the early lessons, too much attention need not be paid to the
position of the head, but, when the horse understands what is
required of him, the rider must be particularly careful to flex him
in the direction of the leading leg and not to allow him to come
off the bit by raising his head.

The correct aids for the canter, with near foreleg leading, are
to sit down in the saddle, draw the right leg back and press the

horse forward with the seat and both legs. As the training advances the right leg may be less drawn back. When the off foreleg is leading, the aids must be reversed.

On no account should one try to obtain a collected canter during the early stages of training; let the canter be free and unconstrained with the horse carrying himself and going well forward. Particular attention must always be paid to the transition back to the trot; there should be no propping or concussion, the horse should be going freely into the trot without any apparent reduction of pace. Plenty of transitions should be made from halt to walk, to trot, to canter and back again. Gradually the period of trotting can be reduced until the horse will go straight from walk to canter and finally from halt to canter and back to halt.

When the true canter is well established on both reins, the counter-canter, that is cantering to the left with the off foreleg leading and vice versa, may be practised. Start by making a small loop from the wall to the wall (as was done at the trot) and gradually increase the depth of the loop until it comes well out into the centre of the school. When this can be achieved without the horse changing his legs, losing his balance or increasing the pace, the rider can try changing the rein at the canter, hold the counter-canter round the short end of the school and then change the rein back again to the true canter. The horse's head must remain bent in the direction of the leading leg throughout.

The counter-canter is an excellent balancing and suppling exercise and very important for obtaining true changes of leg. This balance and suppleness is invaluable in a jumper.

THE REIN-BACK

This should not be attempted until the horse is completely between the rider's hand and leg. The horse must be pressed forward by the rider's legs into a fixed hand when, finding no outlet for the impulsion produced, he will step backwards and should move forward immediately as soon as the hand is relaxed. The backward movement must be absolutely straight, and the steps, by pairs of diagonals, must be of equal length. On no account must the horse be allowed to run back out of hand, or drag his hind feet along the ground, but fore and hind feet must be clearly picked up to an equal height in two-time. In this movement the head may be slightly lowered, but on no account must it be raised. The horse must never be pulled back by the reins.

JUMPING

As soon as the horse will respond to the aids of the legs and the hand, will go freely in the three paces and will turn easily at the indication of the rein, jumping should be combined with the dressage. As when on the lunge, this jumping must be looked upon as a suppling and obedience exercise. Its main object must be to teach the horse to look on jumping as a natural part of his ordinary work and to teach him to jump quietly, without any fuss or bother, over any object that comes in his path. The jumps must be kept low, not more than 2 ft. 6 in. high, and he must learn to jump them without increasing his pace and to resume the same pace again immediately on landing.

CAVALETTIS

These are poles about 10 ft. long fixed to cross bars and so made that by turning them over they will be different heights.

Commence with two poles at the lowest height and 3 to 4 ft. apart. Make the horse walk over them. If he tries to jump the two, put them further apart then, with a little patience, he will soon learn to walk over them. Then put them 4 ft. apart and let him trot over them quietly. As soon as he can do this, gradually increase the number of poles up to six or more, and later increase the distance to 5 ft.

The rider should do this exercise with a loose rein to allow the horse to lower his head, and his aids should not differ from those he would employ if he was trotting over level ground. The horse must retain the same pace and rhythm and, should he lose it, must on no account be taken over the poles again until it is re-established. Between jumping the poles one carries on with the ordinary dressage exercises at the trot.

FIG. E. *Cavaletti, showing how by turning ends it is possible to vary heights of pole*

When the horse performs this exercise smoothly and quietly, maintaining the same pace and cadence both approaching the poles and after, he can be asked to jump other small obstacles such as small parallel bars, a few bricks of a wall, a low gate leaning well away and a small bush fence. This work must still be performed out of the trot and the horse brought quietly back to the trot after the jump. Parallel bars are a most important type of jump at this stage as they make the horse stretch himself and perform a correct parabola.

JUMPING FROM THE CANTER

So far all jumping has been done from the trot at which pace the horse always meets the fence right. When jumping from the canter, owing to the increased length of stride, he will often find himself meeting the fence wrong. This will necessitate the horse either standing back from the fence or putting in a short stride. At this early stage this may, by upsetting the horse's balance, be inclined to excite him or start him jumping in the wrong style.

5. Saddles of honour. In 1965 twenty-one-year-old Alison Westwood, on The Maverick, won saddles of honour as leading rider at five international horse-shows. She was also third in the Ladies World Championship.

6a & b. Harvey and Harvester. Britain's outstanding combination of Harvey Smith and Mr. B. Cleminson's Harvester, three times winner of The John Plater Trophy, the richest prize at the Royal International Horse Show.

It is also liable to disturb the rider's own balance and cause him to interfere with the horse, which may destroy confidence. To prevent this and to get the horse in the habit of meeting the fence right, the following exercises may be recommended.

Place two cavelettis at the second height, 9 ft. apart. Trot into the first one which, being too high to trot over comfortably, the horse will jump and so find himself in the right place to take off for the next one. Next raise the cavalettis to their full height and, still trotting up to the first one, gradually increase their number up to six. Continue the exercise at the canter and trot between the jumping, and on no account jump again if the horse is showing any signs of excitement. The distance between the cavalettis can be increased to 12 or 13 ft., depending on the horse. Another good exercise is to vary the distance between them so that he will have to increase or shorten his stride in order to negotiate them.

Other small fences may be jumped in the same way by placing a cavaletti, at the second height, 9 ft. in front of the fence. When the horse jumps these without any signs of excitement, the distance of the cavaletti can be increased to 18 and 27 ft.; this will require the horse to take at first one and then two in full canter strides before jumping the fence and meeting it right.

The great object of these exercises is to get the horse to jump quietly with a lowered head and rounded back, to maintain the same pace and cadence both coming into the fence and afterwards, and to enjoy jumping. For this reason it is most important that the rider does not interfere with the horse's mouth. Therefore, unless the rider is absolutely sure of his balance over a fence, he should ride with a neckstrap which he can hold. This consists of a stirrup leather or other strap fastened around the horse's neck. Nothing is easier than to catch a horse in the mouth, especially when he takes off sooner than expected. If the rider makes this mistake several times, a young horse will soon start refusing or jumping in bad form, that is with his head up and a hollow back.

To summarize this important aspect of basic training:

EARLY TRAINING (I)

Do not start the jumping mounted until the horse is really confirmed in a well-balanced trot and canter, and is obedient to hand and leg.

Approach every fence at these well-balanced paces and do not jump again until this balanced trot has been re-established.

At any sign of excitement or disinclination to jump, go back to smaller fences.

Mix simple dressage in between the jumping. Practice standing still in front of a jump and after jumping it.

During this stage no fence over 2 ft. 6 in. high or 4 ft. wide should be jumped.

Sit absolutely still and try to get the horse to jump these small fences without giving any more aids than you would to keep him trotting or cantering.

If the horse is in fairly good condition to commence with, four or five months should be sufficient to establish him in this work and prepare him to go on to his proper training for show jumping, combined training or for whatever may be required of him. The owner will find that the care and patience put into this preliminary work will pay him a high dividend in the soundness and future work of his horse.

It may be thought that a disproportionate amount of space has been devoted to this simple basic training on the ground. But having had first-hand experience of the enormous amount of time that the greatest riders in the world put in on this aspect of training I have absolutely no doubt of the importance of it. Indeed I would go so far as to say that the rider who skimps the training on the ground is denying himself the opportunity of reaching the top. With a good natural jumper he may get so far, but he will ultimately be lacking in the equipment necessary to jump an Olympic course or an international 5 ft. course against the clock. He will be lacking the initial training on which all subsequent training is based.

CHAPTER VI

Early Training (II)

I n the previous chapter we have dealt with the first two stages of training; training on the ground, known as dressage, and schooling over little jumps. We now come to the third stage, and perhaps this is best explained by referring now to 'fences' as opposed to 'jumps'.

At this stage the horse is introduced to different types of fences. They are never big, of course, because to overface a horse in these early days will quickly destroy all his confidence; it could even turn him permanently sour.

The fences, nevertheless, should be varied; in fact, the stranger and more varied they are, the better, as a horse will then never be surprised at any fence he encounters, however unusual its appearance. It is for this reason that a young jumper should if possible be taken out hunting. Not only will he meet every kind of obstacle, but he will also learn to look after himself, because so often he will have to jump fences at different angles or from bad take-offs. The reason why Irish horses are so often the best jumpers is because they have been introduced at an early age to hunting over banks and the wild Irish countryside, which is the ideal schooling ground for a jumper, encouraging him to be really clever with his feet.

On the home schooling ground, however, it is at this stage that a horse will meet for the first time walls, brightly coloured poles, logs, rustic stiles, gates and even more fanciful fences such as hay-racks, water troughs and so on: possibly even a water jump itself.

Once he has become used to jumping anything, always controlled and collected, from either direction and, of course, in a different sequence, then a little course can be laid out for him. It must be emphasized, however, that, at this stage, the courses should always be small.

It is quite a good idea to take a horse, after he has done his work on the flat, over a proper course of some ten or twelve fences; this course can be jumped several times, but not too often lest he is just jumping the fences from memory, whereas he should, of course, all the time be having to concentrate on the next fence. This is not only good for his concentration, it also keeps him interested; it is essential that a show jumper should never suffer from boredom, or lose interest. Once he takes jumping for granted then quickly he will start anticipating; as soon as he meets a really difficult course he will, of course, come unstuck. It naturally follows from this that he is no longer obedient to the rider and, before long, the rider will have quite lost control. One sees this so frequently in the show ring, especially in the junior classes where a rider is carted round the course at great speed, doing little else than steering—and not always that! He is certainly having no part in the placing and positioning of his horse as it approaches a fence. Not surprisingly it is difficult for a horse to jump accurately under these conditions.

It cannot be repeated too often that, unless a horse is jumping in a controlled and balanced manner, it will always jump inaccurately and carelessly.

It is, of course, very easy to overdo this simple schooling over fences. It is necessary, therefore, to confine oneself to three or four rounds over the little course of fences that has been prepared, and then to go off for a ride round the roads or even a canter in the fields. Something to take the horse's mind off the simple jumping—otherwise the monotony of it will force him to lose interest.

It is for this reason that the invention of the Foxhunter jumping competitions a few years ago has been such a benefit to British show jumping. The idea of these competitions, instigated by Colonel Harry Llewellyn whose famous horse, Foxhunter, did perhaps more for the sport than any other horse who ever lived, was to introduce new horses and new riders to show jumping. It was felt that there was a certain resistance amongst people who took part in other equestrian sports, against show jumping; people who hunted, or who went in for one-day and three-day events, or who played polo, seemed to take little interest in show jumping, as they felt it was an artificial sport. In fact, they felt perhaps that it was a little too professional, and the jumps were rather too big!

To counteract this, Colonel Llewellyn introduced a competition for complete beginners; the courses were to be over simple fences and only at the second jump-off was the time element introduced. This meant that young and inexperienced horses were not hurried against the clock—nothing unsettles a young horse quicker than to be hurried before it is ready.

The Foxhunter competitions, generously sponsored first by the *Evening Standard* and then by the *Daily Express*, immediately caught on, and an enormous number of new recruits to show jumping were encouraged to 'have a go'. Very quickly the thinning ranks of the established show jumpers were increased and new names, both of riders and horses, quickly appeared on the scenes. Many of the best known jumpers today first appeared in Foxhunter competitions and, but for this new competition for beginners, they might never have come into the sport.

The feature of these Foxhunter competitions is that the courses are straightforward, entirely without traps and therefore comparatively easy, but they are over proper show-jumping fences—poles, planks, gates, walls and so on. It is the weaning, for the horse that has only been hunting, from natural fences of hunting field to the unnatural fences that are a feature of show jumping today.

But there is a very real additional advantage. By taking a horse to a show to take part in a Foxhunter competition, one is introducing a horse to all the sights and sounds of the show ground. It is his introduction to the atmosphere that inevitably surrounds this now very popular sport, with its big crowds and bustling activity. Understandably a horse takes a little time to get used to all this; so often in the past a horse who jumped well enough over his schooling fences at home made a complete nonsense of the fences at the first show he went to, simply because he was distracted by all the noise and the sights going on around him in the show ground. By taking a horse to a small show and entering it for a Foxhunter competition it is given the opportunity to get used to these sights and sounds before ever it jumps in a big competition.

More than that, it is a useful variation of jumping being away from the home ground; it is quite remarkable how a new environment can completely alter and affect a horse. In his own established environment he can be easy, docile, obedient; but suddenly he goes to a new environment and all that he has learnt seems to go out of his head. Again and again one hears a distracted owner complaining that he cannot understand why his horse, that performs so well at home—and this is not only in jumping classes but in ordinary show classes as well—suddenly makes a complete fool of itself when it appears in public.

One can imagine how greatly this is intensified when a horse, for the first time, jumps in an indoor arena with its almost electric atmosphere compared with the comparative calm of the outside. It is for this reason that the Foxhunter Championship Final, which is held at Wembley at the Horse of the Year Show, now has a preliminary 'welcoming' class, the morning of the competition, so that the horses have the chance to get used to jumping indoors in that famous arena before the actual final; so often, before this extra competition was introduced, good horses failed completely because they were quite incapable of the necessary concentration to jump a course of fences in a very much smaller arena than they were used to—to say nothing of the distractions of the huge crowds at very close proximity, and the strange, echoing noises which are inevitably associated with indoor jumping.

Some of this may seem rather far-fetched, and not entirely to do with show jumping; but in fact the psychological side of jumping is almost as important as the physical. I have no hesitation in saying that some of the most successful riders today—

EARLY TRAINING (II)

particularly among our brilliant young lady riders—owe almost all their success to the importance they attach to the psychological approach. This involves getting the horse and the rider in the right frame of mind; conversely, again and again one has seen really good riders, on top-class horses, failing at the crucial moment because their psychological approach is wrong. Obviously it is invidious to mention names, but I can remember at least two occasions on which a top prize at the Royal International Horse Show at the White City was thrown away simply because the rider, with the prize within his graps, panicked at the last fence; if he had kept his head and approached it as if it were any other fence in any ordinary competition, he almost certainly would have cleared it and won the competition; but on each of the two occasions of which I am thinking his anxiety obviously communicated itself to his horse and, on one occasion, the horse crashed through the fence, and on the other occasion, the rider allowed the horse to become so unbalanced approaching the water jump, which was the last fence, that it took off a full stride too early and landed well in the water for 4 vital faults. Obviously a rider is going to feel a nervous tension in a big competition—so is a horse, especially a young and inexperienced horse. The more, therefore, a young horse can be taken round the shows, jumped in small Foxhunter and Grade 'C' competitions, the sooner it will settle down mentally; in addition, of course, it will be getting the necessary muscles more and more into the correct physical condition.

Match-winning temperament is a curious thing; it is a combination of the will to win—indeed, an insistence on winning—and a calm and controlled temperament. There is little doubt that much of Harvey Smith's remarkable success in show jumping is due to the fact that he possesses this priceless match-winning temperament; he is never overawed by the great occasion, and yet he is more determined than any rider in the field that he is going to win. Not surprisingly, he has had, during the past few years, phenomenal success.

It is worth remembering, however, that he is just as painstaking in seeing that his horses, too, have match-winning

71

temperament. Somehow he manages to communicate to them the urgency and the importance of the occasion, and so he is enabled to take extraordinary risks, turning where no one else dare turn to save precious seconds in a jump-off against the clock; again and again, despite the sharpness of his turn the horse, encouraged by Harvey, will make the supreme effort to jump a big fence almost from a standstill—and succeed in doing so: his will to win has communicated itself to his horse.

But it is just as much at his home and on his schooling ground that he teaches his horses this match-winning temperament. He encourages them to be confident and sensible; it may be that his own North-country temperament is of great help to him in this. In addition his horses are always well cared for, well fed and in beautiful condition: they come into the ring looking a picture— a sure sign of top-class horse-mastership.

This is not always so with jumpers. Occasionally one sees a horse in poor condition, which not surprisingly does not jump very well. Occasionally, too, one sees a top-class horse off-colour; it will be observed all too quickly that he is off form as well.

The third phase in the training of a show jumper, then, is the mental and physical approach to jumping fences of a show-jumping type, both at home and in the ring, with an emphasis on the importance of temperament and psychology. This brings us to the fourth and last stage, which is, of course, the jumping of the bigger fences, as in Grade 'A' or top-class competitions.

As will be seen in a later chapter, very few leading jumpers believe in practising over big fences at home. They find by experience that the 'occasion' is enough to make a horse give just that little bit extra to jump a 5-ft. fence as opposed to the 4-ft. fence over which it has practised at home; to clear a 6-ft. spread as opposed to the 4 ft. 6 in. spread it has been jumping in its own schooling ground. The reasons for this are obvious: without the sense of occasion—the atmosphere which affects the rider just as much as the horse—there is always the chance that the horse will not jump quite so well in his own paddock; partly because he has become a little bored with it; partly because

EARLY TRAINING (II)

he has jumped the fences before—often: and he may, there-fore, hit a fence, fall even, and hurt himself. Nobody wants a horse hurt unnecessarily. The top riders, therefore, prefer to school over smaller fences, concentrating on the particular kind of fence for which the horse has a weakness, i.e. spread fences, a wall, or even a water jump.

It is in the ring that the horse is really getting his experience, and, indeed, in a busy show-jumping season, when horses are travelling from show to show two and even three times a week, there is little enough time for schooling, such schooling as there is, being done in the practice ring at the show, when a colleague or an assistant helps with a practice fence.

Once a horse has reached the top there is no reason why he should not stay there with a minimum of practising over fences; it will be found that most of the top riders spend all their prac-tice time in working on the ground; that is to say, in simple dressage which will keep the horse fit, supple and obedient, so that the approach to the fence can be properly controlled, for it is, of course, in the approach that the horse either succeeds or fails when it comes to big fences. Jumping today, with the standard so high, is so much a question of accuracy that it can make all the difference if a horse takes off as little as 6 in. too near to, or too far from, the fence; and, when it comes to com-binations, it is even more imperative that the horse should land exactly the right distance from the first part, so that he has sufficient space for the right-sized stride to take him to the take-off for the second part; all this is gained from disciplining a horse, making him supple and obedient, rather than practising over big fences.

Most people will have heard, or have read, of the various rumours of malpractices in training methods, but these will be dealt with in a later chapter. Suffice it to say that the top jumpers have found from their own experience that they will only reach the top—and stay at the top—by the sort of training methods that have been described in this and the previous chapter.

CHAPTER VII

The Top Twenty

One might have entitled this chapter 'straight from the horse's mouth', except that it is the top riders who are speaking rather than the horses.

It seemed to me that in a book such as this it might be of unusual interest to hear from some of the top riders themselves, as to what they consider to be the priorities in training and schooling a high-class show jumper. Accordingly I approached those who can generally be considered the leading twenty riders, all of whom I am privileged to regard as friends; though obviously opinions will differ and some will feel that certain names which have been omitted should have been included, and vice versa.

All promptly and readily responded—with one exception whose identity the reader must guess for himself!—and I herewith produce their contributions with brief biographical notes, and a few comments.

They are purposely in no particular order.

GEORGE HOBBS

A Sussex farmer, George Hobbs was well-known as a professional steeplechase jockey until he took up show jumping seriously, though in fact he had competed as a junior before the war.

George Hobbs is a great character and very popular both with the public and his fellow competitors. He always has plenty to say at the B.S.J.A. A.G.M. being a barrack-room lawyer of the most attractive, amusing and valuable kind: hence his generous contribution that follows.

Three times he has been second in the King George V Cup at the Royal International Horse Show, but perhaps his greatest achievement was the Ronson Trophy, the Victor Ludorum at the Horse of the Year Show in 1964, on Royal Lord the 15 h.h. huntservant's horse that had won the *Daily Express* Foxhunter Championship ten years earlier.

I personally prefer a horse that is a little over-couraged and needs a little time to mature and settle, although there are plenty of examples of nervous horses, that providing they have a big jump to start with, gain in courage as they mature.

I do not believe in wasting time on a horse that does not possess a big natural jump, as all the schooling and dressage in the world will not put there what he was not born with.

Schooling will only help one to obtain and use to one's best advantage what Nature had already put there in the first place.

I do not believe that dressage or training on the flat wants carrying to too advanced a stage. Teach the horse to ride balanced and relaxed, answering to aids, changing legs and turning, quickening and slowing to the rider's commands without undue argument is what is required. To try to regiment a jumper beyond this stage has a tendency to destroy a horse's natural initiative, and I do not think that there is a rider born that will not need his horse's assistance and help somewhere around today's complicated courses.

Elaborate jumps are not particularly necessary, but initiative is. Straw bales, oil drums, plastic sheets, a little ditch dug in front of jumps, enable a horse to approach whatever his rider puts him at with confidence. Good poles in firm cups that give a horse a sharp reminder if he does not pay attention. In my opinion one should never school a horse over fixed fences, as I believe that unnecessary falls are not only dangerous to rider and run a high risk of injury to the horse that one has spent a lot of time on, but also produce horses that when they are in trouble at big spreads, panic, shut their eyes, scramble and before long become regular fallers. It is far more effective to use an oak slat about 1 in. thick by about 2 in. wide the same height as the obstacle that one is schooling over, about a foot back on the take-off side.

Finally, having found and schooled a good young horse, take the trouble to find a piece of good going to work it on whenever humanly possible, thus preventing or at least delaying the onset of navicular, ringbone and general foot injuries.

It was particularly unfortunate that George Hobbs missed most of the 1967 season through injury from a fall when schooling—not over fixed fences!

One feels that his schooling is based on sound common sense and experience, but that he is not over sold on the value of dressage.

DAVID BROOME

Amongst the riders themselves it is generally agreed that David Broome has no superior as a show jumper with the exception of Harvey Smith, whose style nevertheless is entirely different. He is the eldest of a remarkably talented family, with a father who is a near genius in anything to do with horses.

David Broome competed in both the Rome and Tokyo Olympic Games winning a bronze medal at the former with Sunsalve in 1960, the year in which he was European Champion, as he was also in 1967. He has also twice won the King George V Gold Cup. In 1967 he won the National Championship.

He is a rider who believes in 'going on', has a wonderful sense of timing and beautiful hands. Any horse goes for him and as well as on the great horses with which he has been associated, such as Sunsalve and Mister Softee, he has won as much if not more on very moderate horses.

A horse must have a good jump in it to start with.

The first priority, then, is to get a good mouth on a horse.

One of my best horses needed a 12 ft. wall in front of it to make it turn to the left. On several occasions I needed two hands on one rein to turn him.

It's no good if a horse lies heavy on the bit, so somehow you've got to get the mouth right, and it can only be done with time and patience.

Then one must get him balanced correctly. This needs time, too, and patience.

The most difficult part in jumping is the approach. As long as you can keep the horse on the bit you should be all right, but it's not easy.

If you can get your horse angling himself approaching the fence at the right pace, or on the right stride, with his back-end under him and a proper contact on the bit then you are getting somewhere.

One feels that David rides and schools almost by instinct, as perhaps all great natural horsemen do. For him what really counts is control. Perfect timing is only possible if there is complete control, hence the importance of the mouth. If the approach is right everything else falls into place.

His control and judgment were never better exemplified than at the Rome Olympics in 1960 when he cleared the 16-ft. water jump and then turned at 90 deg. to clear a big set of parallels six strides away, something no other rider achieved.

DOUGLAS BUNN

As founder and director of the All England Jumping Course at Hickstead, Douglas Bunn has made a great contribution to show jumping since the war; but for a good many years he has also been at the top as a rider.

Though he is particularly associated with Beethoven, an Irish-bred horse he brought to the top in 1964 and on which he won the Grand Prix at the Toronto Winter Fair in 1965 and was runner-up for the King George V Gold Cup the same year, he started his adult jumping career immediately after the war. When he was still an undergraduate he was second in the 1946 Victory Championship.

Beethoven was another *Daily Express* Foxhunter winner (1962) and is one of Britain's most consistent international horses. Frequently during the last few years Douglas Bunn has captained the British Team.

The two main qualities required of a jumper are that he should be able to jump higher and wider than most other horses and that he should be obedient to ride.

His athletic ability should be apparent almost from the beginning, although with a young horse it will take time to find out what he is really capable of and whether he has the class to be a force in international competition. Loose schooling is useful at the beginning because it enables the trainer to get him jumping over a variety of obstacles without the distraction of a rider on his back. Moreover, the horse at this stage may not be sufficiently well broken for the rider to be of any great assistance to him. But it does introduce the horse to jumping. Loose schooling can save one the trouble of continuing with a horse that really is not good enough. In advanced training loose schooling is of no value and it is wrong to think that a horse will not make a mistake when jumping loose. He probably will not all the time see the problems posed are straightforward but I can build a few fences in a loose school to catch any horse, whereas if that horse had the help of a good rider, and would listen to him, he would probably jump the fence without fault. The next stage is to start work on the flat. There is no mystery about good ground work. Keep riding him right and he will eventually go right. This is the quickest way in the long run and will save many vexations. The horse should stop, go, turn, with the various shades between these movements, on command; and he should do so calmly. It is amazing how many horses one sees that will not do this, even in their own paddocks when they are not stimulated by competition. Always do something positive during a nagging session—not just ride about aimlessly at one pace. Some horses have a 'built in' disobedience (like a kick back!) which is usually caused by too much courage or just plain nerves. It is unwise to try and iron this out too quickly—compromise, learn to live with it, and hope that time will bring an improvement. A lot of our best horses which are highly trained in dressage rarely make top-class performers. They are too obedient, and have no initiative.

Practise at home over all the types of obstacles and situations you are likely to meet in the arena, but not with the fences at full height. A competitive horse will find the extra height on the day. Once a young horse is used to the arena, iron out any snags at home, not in the ring. Avoid tricky course builders. They can set a young horse back for months. When you think a horse knows his job, try to fool him occasionally, for example, by standing back a little too far or coming in a little too close. But at all times keep him so that he can be ridden with great precision, when it is needed. There are occasions, such as in the Nations' Cups, etc., when it is precision all the way, and lesser-trained horses and less-skilled riders find themselves in trouble despite the fact that they win in their turn.

As one might expect from an expert course builder, Douglas Bunn is something of a theorist, but a practical one. Like George Hobbs he is suspicious of too much dressage, but believes in common sense work on the ground.

His reference to Beethoven's kick back is interesting. Nizefela first caught the fancy of the public with his kick back, as later did Vibart; it seems almost to be part of horses of exceptional strength as Nizefela, Vibart and Beethoven all are.

PETER ROBESON

Though still under forty, Peter Robeson must be considered

as one of the veterans of show jumping: almost an elder states-
man.

He first represented Britain back in 1949 with his famous
mare Craven A, on which he won most of the biggest international prizes, and was twice reserve in the Olympic Games.
Latterly he has had remarkable success, including an Olympic
Bronze Medal at Tokyo with Firecrest, on which he also won
the 1967 King George V Gold Cup.

Peter Robeson is a perfectionist, a classic horseman who has
won the admiration of the greatest judges of horsemanship all
over the world. He is infinitely patient, being quite content, for
instance, to take four years in bringing Firecrest to Olympic
standard. Equally he is content to be selective in choosing the
shows at which he competes. No rat race all round Britain from
one show to another for him.

'If an hoss don't ride 'e don't jump.'

This I heard from a wise horsey character before the war.
At that time I was too young to understand what he meant.
The longer I live the more I realize how true this saying is. The
basis of good jumping, in my belief, is a high standard of
elementary dressage, plus hunting where the horse's character
is suitable, in order to obtain complete balance and co-
ordination of the horse's movement. In most instances
cavalettis are the best introduction to show jumping. These
and dressage, plus hunting for a reasonably limited period,
should be considered in the same light as an athlete uses his
training and gymnasium in order to obtain supple co-ordination and peak fitness.

To be able to produce a jumper in top competitions which
goes boldly and confidently it is essential to build up a partnership between horse and rider in every possible way. Time is
the most important element in this, and here there is no short
cut. The use of cavalettis, figure of eighting, multiple small
combinations of the type he is likely to meet, small waters
increasing in size, within reason, are all exercises which increase the horse's knowledge and confidence. In concluding, I

7. Returning with a smile. Alan Oliver, on Mr. Cawthraw's Sweep, back at the top after a spell in the wilderness.

8. Looking forward. The young John Kidd on the threshold of top international honours after his Leipzic Grand Prix victory on Millstream and other big successes representing Britain.

should like to stress how important it is to treat every horse as an individual. From these basic ideas one hopes to achieve some measure of success and a great amount of pleasure.

These two simple paragraphs speak for themselves. They make all too clear his priorities, but unlike so many, Peter Robeson practises exactly what he preaches.

SEAMUS HAYES

There are few more popular riders in Show Jumping than Seamus Hayes, the only non-British rider I have included. He has become so much part of the British scene that though he comes from Ireland his inclusion seems justified.

His father was responsible for buying from the Irish Army many of the horses that became so famous between the wars, but after the war it was riding in the North of England that Seamus Hayes first showed his great ability. Riding for Mr. Makin he was very much part of these early Horse of the Year Shows at Harringay, many of his brilliant performances against the clock being unforgettable, not wholly preparing one, however, for the almost perfect horseman that he was to become riding for Ireland.

He has gained successes all over the world, has twice won the Hickstead Derby and has established with Goodbye a unique and delightful partnership.

As cheerful in defeat as in victory he epitomizes all that is best in show jumping.

In outlining my priorities in training show jumpers I must state here that my aims have always been to acquire perfection. Consequently my methods and techniques have changed from time to time.

My success up until 1957, I credit to a large amount of natural ability and certain know how which my late father instilled in me. (He learnt it from Col. P. Rodzianko.)

Since 1957 I began to take more notice of written theory. With the wonderful help in 1963 by Mr. R. Hall (Fulmer), in understanding of the correct elementary training and the application of it at all times, I now feel that perfection is in sight.

My future results in international competitions, with a number of different horses in show jumping and eventing will be the guide, as to whether I am achieving any good.

My method at the moment is as follows.

1st. Controlled forward impulsion. The difficulty here is to be sure that the horse is working his inside hind leg and not conning the rider. If the hind leg is active the horse will not lie on the outside hard.

2nd. Even rhythm in all paces. The use of the *voice*, slow when the horse is in a hurry (Wo Ho!) and fast (Come on!) when the horse gets slow, is a big help in acquiring rhythm.

3rd. Correct bend in all movements. This is easily achieved if the well written aids are used at all times.

The rider's balance must be perfect to carry out the above and he must never lose his temper, controlling his feelings, (relaxed and active) at all times.

When jumping, the rider must leave the judgment of the take-off to the horse, the rider controlling the pace and direction, and maintaining the rhythm.

The horse must be taught (like a child) to follow the rider's will (obedience) and must never be bullied, returning to his stable in a happy frame of mind.

A fascinating contribution. Obviously with experience the value of theory has superseded the natural ability. With exceptional skill and immense dedication Seamus Hayes shows that he is able to combine theory with practice. Obviously sold on dressage—Mr. Robert Hall is one of the greatest experts in the world—he yet appreciates the value of the voice (Wo ho! and Come on!) and still believes that the judgment of the take-off must be left to the horse. After all it is the horse that is doing the jumping.

THE TOP TWENTY

TED WILLIAMS

In an even more pronounced and remarkable way than Seamus Hayes, Ted Williams has changed his style to great effect, though his change has been more associated with the type of horses he now rides compared with those with which he was earlier associated, than in actual riding methods.

Already well known before the war he immediately after the war became a doyen of the B.S.J.A. with which he was more closely associated than international competition. His horses, Sunday Morning, Pegasus, Yorkshireman were essentially B.S.J.A. horses—he won the B.S.J.A. spurs at The Horse of the Year show five times. Then in 1963 he started riding, for Mr. Frank Smith of Leicester, two South American-bred horses purchases from Nelson Pessoa. This was something of a revolution for him, but within weeks he had established himself completely with his new style horses, and he is now harder to beat than at any time in his career.

This is rather a difficult task, because there is so much to knowing a horse. However, I will try and point out the most important aspects in training show jumpers.

First of all, a horse *must* have natural jumping ability to make a first-class show jumper. I find my problems with young horses is finding this out as soon as possible, so that months and months of schooling are not wasted.

Always get to know your horse's character; I talk to my horses as much as possible as in this way they gain confidence in their rider.

Any young horses I get are lunged quietly for half an hour to settle them down before riding for about fifteen to twenty minutes; then I take them over poles on the ground and small cavalettis. After a few days, I get the horse to walk and trot quietly over larger cavalettis and usually carry on this procedure for two or three weeks.

83

The next lesson is lunging over a jump about 1 ft. high, gradually increasing the height to assess his capabilities. In my experience, after two weeks the horse should be jumping 4 ft. and is then capable of schooling on for a show jumper.

I then start to ride him over small jumps, just set anywhere, not bothering about distances, so he learns to look after himself a little, and can make his own arrangements when meeting the fence wrong.

All the time I am trying to get to know my horse's character, his likes, his dislikes—no two horses are the same; some are inclined to be more nervous than others and certain things will soon upset them. A horse should never resent being asked to do anything within his capabilities.

With a made horse that is bought for me to keep and ride, the procedure is very much the same, I still have to get to know the horse and his particular ways, and also try to teach him my ways too; as, again, no two riders are the same.

I have found with experience that if I get a horse worked up, the best thing is to stop riding and take him back to his stable until later in the day, or possibly the next day. No horse will concentrate if you get on the wrong side of him.

With ready-made horses, I find it more difficult to get to know their ways than with a young horse. Sometimes I find it difficult when riding several horses in the same competition, I have to concentrate very hard to think of each horse's little ways, and at times do make mistakes thinking that I am on another horse.

It takes a lot of experience to know what to do when you find yourself in trouble, and it takes a very good horse to get you out of it. These of course are the best horses, and are what I call show jumpers!

I find the Argentinian horses are very quick thinkers, and I have to think quickly as well. A good horse is rather like a fast car, and if you are not able to think quickly you are soon in trouble.

In summing up, a horse must have ability to jump, the right temperament, courage and ability to think for himself.

THE TOP TWENTY

The emphasis on knowing the horse's character is most interesting. The principles are basic, down to earth, as one would expect with Ted Williams— but essentially sympathetic. Note the value attached to the use of the voice again, and how interesting the summing up of the Argentinian horses.

JEAN GOODWIN

Jean Goodwin won the B.S.J.A. Ladies National Championship at Windsor in 1967. Although she had been there or thereabouts ever since she was promoted from junior classes it was her victory in the Puissance at the Royal International in 1966 that really established her as one of our leading lady riders, a success which lead to her being included in our British Team at Dublin a few weeks later.

Preparing a horse to fulfil the present day jumping season which is extremely exacting and strenuous requires complete fitness, and to achieve this it is a necessary minimum to cover three essentials: (1) Feeding, (2) Road Work, and (3) Schooling or Ground Work.

Feeding, as with human beings, plays a very important role in keeping the horse fit and well throughout the season. No hard and fast rules can be laid down, but a balanced diet is essential and attention must be paid to the individual reaction of the horse, and can usually be judged by the temperament or response of the horse. The usual feed of the average horse consists of oats, bran and a small amount of good hay. Vitamins are useful to give a completely balanced diet; this will be varied from time to time according to the amount of work the horse is required to do.

The first stage of actual training consists of road work and this is most important, and normally lasts between one to two hours each day and comprises steady walking, preferably part of which is climbing hills; this helps to tone and harden the muscles and improves the stamina.

The schooling or ground work varies according to the experience and age of the horse. There are many different ideas and techniques of schooling young horses but they all have one objective—obedience. In this present day with very big courses and different distances between fences it is very important to teach the horse to lengthen and shorten his stride. Also remembering that time is an important factor in the final stage of most classes, it is necessary to have free forward movement and to be able to control the pace of the horse. For this the horse must be schooled, with changes of pace and direction and generally making sure that the horse is between hand and leg while maintaining balance.

Cavalettis and jumping small obstacles help the young horse, as in the approach and over the cavalettis he learns to lower and stretch his neck thus preparing himself to bascule and jump in the correct way. By doing these exercises he also develops rhythm and learns to synchronize his stride.

With a Grade 'A' or a more experienced horse a great deal of schooling is not necessary as this should have been done in his initial stages of his career. The experienced horse is rarely ever jumped at home as normally the horse is jumping regularly at shows and requires a change of work. The only time that this type of horse is jumped is to correct a fault. Over jumping can have the opposite effect to that desired.

Training if carried out correctly is well worth the time and effort and should be designed to build confidence and coordination between horse and rider. If time and care are not devoted to this objective, the horse will be unable to obtain optimum performance, and this can only lead to lack of confidence and disappointment.

Patience is the keynote here, and a dedicated thoroughness. The insistence on proper feeding is of great interest as a horse off-colour obviously cannot give of his best.

Jean Goodwin's contribution appears to me to underline that there is no luck in the position she holds as Ladies National Champion (1967).

THE TOP TWENTY

ALISON WESTWOOD

Still in her early twenties Alison has certainly scaled the heights, though the very greatest prizes have still eluded her. Twice she has gone near to winning the Queen Elizabeth Cup: she was third in the Ladies World Championship in 1965. On the other hand her great Irish-bred horse The Maverick was the leading horse at no less than five international shows in 1965.

In 1966 when she added the difficult O'Malley to her string she had a less successful year, but when O'Malley went back to Harvey Smith and she was able to concentrate on The Maverick again she was soon back into top form.

Alison Westwood only took up riding because, suffering ill health as a child her doctor suggested that she should take up some pastime that would give her fresh air and exercise.

An exceptionally sympathetic rider, she has got the very best out of The Maverick, a very highly strung horse, and when his turn is over there is little doubt that she will produce another to keep her at the top.

Schooling a young horse, hoping that one day you may have a top-grade horse like The Maverick, in my opinion should never be too hard or boring. Two or three weeks concentrated dressage work should be punctuated by a day's hunting if the horse is of suitable temperament, and if he is likely to hot up and undo all the work you have put in, rides across country and road work are a pleasant change of scenery for him. It is most important that your young horse should always feel fit and well: if he seems to be losing condition after some weeks' work, take a week off and graze him by the roadside for twenty minutes each day and then start working again.

For a young horse with the aptitude for jumping, small well built fences can be jumped even in the very first stages of his training. This is to encourage his natural ability so that as he becomes more balanced he will find that he needs to make less effort to make these jumps. One should not always put fences on completely flat ground: if you have a field with ridge and furrow or even a dip in it, small solid fences up and down or on top of a hump all help to make the horse think for himself. If he is inclined to rush his fences, those slightly awkward places encourage him to steady himself and over the jump he will spend more time in the air, which when you start to jump in the ring is most essential.

You will by this stage begin to know your horse's best and worst points. You must make sure not to over school on the worst points. When he is showing willingness and some improvement, forget it completely and let him do something he enjoys, for he is no different to us humans, too much of one thing will sour him for everything. It is a mistake many people make to try to jump young horses too early in their training, and spoil them. A few shows between schooling is a good idea as the horse becomes used to the noise and people and the different surroundings. If you can, go to a show and just ride round, pop over the practice jumps and get him used to all these things before he eventually jumps in a ring; this is a very good idea.

Most of my ideas are obviously based on a fairly highly strung young horse, which nearly all top-class jumpers are, the excitable temperament giving them the necessary incentive to win when the time comes.

The essence of your training should be to produce a free moving and pleasing spectacle of harmony between horse and rider.

All carefully thought out, practical and sympathetic. This point of never allowing a horse to become bored seems to be especially important. So often horses are over schooled or over jumped, become bored and turn sour. The suggestion of placing practice fences on uneven ground to help make a horse think for himself is particularly interesting.

THE TOP TWENTY

ANDREW FIELDER

Andrew Fielder burst on to the public scene—or screen—in 1962 with his spectacular performances on the mighty Vibart, the bounding horse with a sledge-hammer kick back. Standing 17·2 h.h. Vibart is anything but an easy ride and Andrew Fielder has certainly been brilliant to achieve so much with this anything but easy horse.

In 1964 he won the Leading Show Jumper of the Year title at The Horse of the Year Show, but was too young to be considered for the Olympic Team. Internationally his great success was the Swiss Grand Prix in Geneva in 1965. The following year he became the B.S.J.A. National Champion at The Royal. In 1967 he won the Aachen Grand Prix and the Hamburg Jumping Derby.

There are those who consider Andrew Fielder as a one-horse rider. I do not believe this to be so. It is perhaps truer to say that he is a one type of horse rider. His horses are often strong and headstrong. He loves taming them and challenging their strength.

One cannot set down any hard and fast rules on training a horse for top-class show jumping, as every horse I've ever had has had a totally different temperament, so therefore one must be fairly flexible.

Basically, however, I try to teach the horse firstly obedience through elementary dressage, assuming the animal in question has a good consistent 'Pop'. Depending on the animal of course, this can take some time, and a good deal of patience.

When training a young horse I feel it is essential to keep him happy in his work by frequently changing his routine. I do quite a lot of long-rein work and lunging as it both supples the horse and again teaches him obedience, very necessary for top-class show jumping.

When the horse has had a few months of this training, and

should be quite efficient at different dressage moves, then I start slowly trotting him over small and varied obstacles until the horse begins to gain confidence while still keeping up with the long-reining and lunging and dressage. I then begin to raise the fences and now and again put up a proper little course.

After some time of this sort of training I find a spell in the field does a horse the world of good, freshening him and giving him a new lease of life. When I bring him in again some good hard road work strengthens his leg muscles and generally makes him fit. I am fortunate in as much as my natural surroundings of the Yorkshire Moors help very much in this part of the programme. When I think my horse is really fit and well, I again introduce him to the jumping as before, trotting him to begin with and then very slow cantering, extending and shortening all the time.

Sometimes during the training of a young horse I like to lightly hunt him or take him to a Hunter Trial because the natural surroundings and fences, I think, help to gain his confidence.

By this time the beginning of the season will be approaching and if all the training has gone well, the young Grade 'C' should be ready to start his career in the show jumping ring.

This is illuminating in that Andrew Fielder's approach to a novice is essentially conservative, belying the dramatic performance seen by the public with Vibart: but it must be remembered that Vibart is an exceptional horse, unlike anything else jumping today. Inevitably his partnership with Vibart must influence his performance with others: though the quiet way he handles his young Australian horse, Dixieland, is extremely encouraging.

HARVEY SMITH

There is little doubt that Harvey Smith is the outstanding figure in British Show Jumping today. He is certainly a prolific winner. With a great determination, an immensely valuable will to win, he is difficult to beat, especially on the big occasion.

Self-taught, but with a great natural ability, he first came to the fore on Farmers Boy, a horse he bought out of a draft from Ireland. He has succeeded on horses as different as the 17 h.h. Harvester and 15·2 h.h. South African-bred Sea Hawk. He alone has achieved the full potential of the Canadian-bred O'Malley. He has taken to the top such horses as the 200 gns. Warpaint and the German Silver King. He has won the John Player Trophy in the International Horse Show four times.

He could perhaps be described as the Fred Trueman of show jumping. Immensely popular with the crowd, single-minded in his approach to the sport, an individualist and sometimes a headache to the organizers, the show-jumping scene is certainly the richer for his presence.

Give away my top secrets? I can't be expected to do that can I? I don't believe all that much in schooling on the ground (dressage): the real priorities are complete obedience and thoroughness. A horse must never be allowed to get away with being careless. That's all there is to it.

Brief and to the point, as one would expect from Harvey Smith; he is a man of few words, and who shall blame him for that? He is in my opinion a genius, and I use the word advisedly, accepting that genius is an infinite capacity for taking pains.

Complete obedience. Perhaps this suggests methods unduly strong-handed. As they are top secret we do not know them; but to anyone who may be dubious I would say 'look at his horses'. Without exception they are always extremely well and happy. Indeed there can be no doubt that Harvey Smith is no less a horsemaster than a horseman.

Thoroughness: and thus he assures his horses being well balanced and temperamentally right. No gags and gadgets for Harvey Smith. All his horses are ridden on a simple snaffle, yet their heads are in the right position and always steady. His spurs are blunted: if he hits a horse it is one sharp smack—what the jockey so aptly describes as a reminder. When he jumped 7 ft. at the Horse of the Year Show a few months after purchasing the cast-off Warpaint I remember his father saying to me: 'It's all been achieved without a stick ever being used.'

The story may be apocryphal, but it was said at the time that when Harvey Smith first acquired Warpaint he had gone sour and had a reputation of being a 'dog'. Harvey took him out for a ride on the moors near his home at Bingley but when he wanted to turn for home Warpaint would not have it. He just stuck his toes in. Harvey just sat there: there was no battle: only occasional persuasion. Six hours later Warpaint walked home, and never gave any further trouble!

To his insistence on obedience and thoroughness could be added determination. There are few more people in any sport who are so utterly determined to win.

It is sometimes said that money is his god and his determination stems from this. I personally do not believe this to be entirely true, though he welcomes 'the brass' and, indeed, remembering the string of horses that he keeps, needs it.

No, rather I believe it to be an inborn will to win, indispensable in any competitive sport if one is to get to the top, and stay there as Harvey Smith does.

The trouble with such determination is that it inevitably leads to an intolerance: of wrong decisions, badly built or designed courses, mistakes, inaccuracies. A character such as Harvey Smith does not suffer fools gladly, and one can but hope that this does not lead to too many clashes with stewards who, understandably, will not tolerate any sort of an 'incident' on the part of a competitor. To repeat Rule 5 (b) 'No member shall conduct himself in a manner which, in the opinion of the discipline authority, is detrimental to the character and/or prejudicial to the interests of the Association and/or show jumping.'

Harvey Smith is the most 'professional' rider in the sport. He is an artist, he is dedicated and he knows exactly what the rider is entitled to expect from the sport. In exchange he gives the public full value for money.

THE TOP TWENTY

ANNELI DRUMMOND-HAY

That Anneli Drummond-Hay is a very fine horsewoman goes without saying. Few riders, male or female have reached the very top of one equestrian sport and then switched to another and within months reached the top of that.

On Merely-a-Monarch Anneli Drummond-Hay won the Three-Day Events at Badminton and Burghley. She then took up show jumping and within months was in top international class. But that remarkable achievement though indicative of her prowess is almost insignificant compared with the wonderful way she has staged a come back.

In 1964 Merely-a-Monarch appeared to be finished. He started refusing, was scarcely ever in the money. Worse than that, he appeared to have lost heart as well as courage. He looked a shadow of his former magnificent self. All his zest for living and jumping, seemed to have evaporated.

With the greatest patience, and determination, Anneli Drummond-Hay nursed and coaxed him back to his former self. By the end of 1967 he had not only reached, but passed his former peak. In 1966 he won the Grand Prix at Toronto. In 1967 his international success was crowned by an invitation to represent Britain in the European Ladies Championship.

If I could train my show jumpers as easily as writing down my methods in a few words, my task would be much simplified. I find each horse so different in ability and character, and consequently their training varies accordingly. Many systems have been used with equal success throughout the world, and I do not think one could describe any one method as being superior to another.

I firmly believe that the most successful horses are the ones that are prepared to accept those particular rider's arrangements, to ensure the all-important partnership. Having begun my riding career in Three-Day Events, I still apply this type

93

of training to my show jumpers. Basically they must be supple and relaxed, balanced and obedient to my hand and leg, which is achieved by dressage on the flat. I try to establish this firmly, so that all is not lost when the added excitement of jumping begins.

For me the success of each jump depends heavily on the quality of the approach. Over the jump I like my horse to bascule, making full use of his head and neck, thus enabling him to take-off at varied distances from the fence. I find trotting over small obstacles very beneficial for this. I seldom school over fences larger than 4 ft. 6 in., but I like to vary the type and spacing rather than the height, to encourage confidence in the horse and to teach him to allow me to readjust his stride where necessary. For handiness I find angling and turning in short to fences helps them as well.

On the whole I am more concerned with how my horse goes than where he finishes. Providing he continues to make progress I am quite happy, and one day, (I hope!) I may be able to reap further rewards.

Like David Broome she emphasizes the importance of the approach. Obviously schooling on the ground, or dressage, plays an important part in training, and it is interesting that like Peter Robeson, the other great believer in classic riding, the perfectionist, she sets more store in how her horse goes rather than winning.

ALTHEA ROGER SMITH

In 1966 on Havana Royal Althea Roger Smith won the Queen Elizabeth Cup at the White City. She thus joins the select and exclusive ranks of Lady Champions. She has frequently represented Great Britain and yet she has never quite achieved the success internationally that she deserves, though few people have jumped double clear rounds in Nations' Cup as she did at Aachen and the White City in 1967.

The real earnest of her success lies in the fact that the horses on which she has succeeded have been horses entirely made by herself and horses, moreover, that might well not have reached the top with any other rider. Further evidence of her outstanding ability is her versatility. In addition to winning in show jumping she has frequently succeeded in One-Day Events.

I find it rather difficult to put down in a few words the training I would give a top-class show jumper.

There are so many different and successful approaches. I personally think a lot depends on the type of horse, taking into consideration his temperament and ability. On the whole I try to give all my horses the same basic ground work, then later vary the training according to each individual horse's personality and ability to learn—some learn quicker than others. I think it is a great mistake to rush them on too quickly. They must have time to absorb everything they are taught. There is so much a jumper has to learn.

The idea I carry in my mind is first to teach a horse to go correctly on the flat—not necessarily at dressage test standard, but enough to enable him eventually to approach and jump correctly very large obstacles in the most economical and effortless way, thus making jumping so much easier for the horse.

I think the most important first stage is to have the horse completely obedient to your hand and leg, never any resistance or stiffening when you want to check or go forward since when in the ring the horse must respond the second he is asked to do anything.

I am a great believer in having a horse completely supple. Some suppling exercises I do on the flat are circling on either rein at a sitting trot or collected canter, varying the size of the circles by gradually decreasing and then increasing the circle, the whole time making the horse move from the leg. Another exercise is 'shoulder-in and -out', which is a two-track movement.

It is important for a horse to flex his hocks and have them

right underneath him when he is jumping. An exercise which I find helps to teach him this is to canter directly from a walk, or from canter to walk or halt.

The jumping exercises I do are all part of teaching the horse to bend and bascule over the fence.

I do a lot of trotting over small fences and cavaletti work, which consists of three or four cavalettis, with a jump of about 2 ft. 6 in. to 3 ft., as the last one. I keep varying the distance between so that the horse has to lengthen or shorten his stride to jump.

All these exercises I do, with all my horses, however experienced. I never school over large fences at home.

A really professional approach, with great attention to detail, the fruits of which are seen in her successes when jumping against the clock over a big course. It may well be that it is this carefully thought out approach to the problems of training that have resulted in her being one of the comparatively few riders who really 'go on' as opposed to 'hooking up'. In other words such is her control that she can adjust her stride in the approach at great speed, and similarly can turn at speed without losing her impulsion.

ALAN OLIVER

Few people in any sport can successfully make the grade from child prodigy to adult star. Alan Oliver has succeeded in doing this, but not without having to face difficulties that many would have found insuperable.

His acrobatic style as a child, helped by an incredible sense of timing, was suited, more or less, to National competitions judged under B.S.J.A. rules, but was not wholly suitable to international jumping with its big spreads and difficult distances. Inevitably this meant a change, or at least a modification of style. This took time, and for some years he had to be content with comparatively limited success. He maintained his position,

9a & b. Irish Wizard I. Seamus Hayes, Ireland's outstanding international rider, on Doneraile, and (*below*) on Mr. McGrath's Goodbye III, twice winner of the Hickstead Jumping Derby.

10. Douglas Bunn, controversial Maestro of Hickstead, on Beethoven, his great Irish-bred horse that won the Foxhunter championship in 1962, and three years later confirmed his international status by winning the Toronto Grand Prix.

largely due to his successes at all levels of national competition, but it was really only with his riding of Sweep—due incidentally to the tragic death of the great north-country rider Chris Jackson—that he really found himself right at the top again. The pleasure felt by his big victory at the 1966 Horse of the Year Show on Mr. Cawthraw's Sweep testifies to his long held popularity, with competitors and public alike. It is hard to believe that it is more than twenty years since he first brought out Red Admiral. After ten years he was recalled to the British team in 1967.

Scope, balance, quick reactions: these must be the priorities for a show jumper. One must always try to get the right sort of experience at the bigger shows. It is of little use, for instance, trying over big spreads at home.

Fences 4 ft. high, with spreads of not more than 4 ft., are quite enough at home. Horses will always try harder in the ring: this is also true of the rider because he is riding for gains.

Plenty of practice at home over small fences especially combinations, but leave the big fences for the ring: I personally do not believe in schooling over water. Ninety-five per cent of those who fail at the water do so because they go too fast and are already slowing when they meet the fence. In fact four or five strides acceleration should be enough.

One should always talk to one's horses, steady them; especially round corners: then they will settle and so keep their energy for jumping.

The ideal qualities in a show jumper are good temperament, scope, responsiveness, quickness and being alert.

It is the good horse than can get you out of trouble.

Alan Oliver makes no bones about 'the gains'. And why not? Jumping in an expensive sport and unless one wins one is soon out of business, except those fortunate enough to be able to indulge in jumping as a hobby. Here is further evidence that the will to win is an essential part of the make-up of any top athlete in any sport.

Obviously Alan Oliver knows what he is about in the training of his horses, as one might expect with a father who has proved himself one of the most able producers of show jumpers in our time.

It is interesting that he, too, believes in the use of his voice.

JOHN AND JANE KIDD

There have been a number of brothers and sisters successful in show jumping at the same time, the Broomes and Barnes being obvious examples, but few have represented Britain both in Junior and Senior events at the same times, as have the Kidds.

Encouraged by their mother who has for some years been an enthusiastic patron of show jumping—she has even established the sport in Barbados—the Kidds have had good horses from an early age and have taken the trouble to learn how to ride them.

John quickly rode to the top where he was promoted to adult classes, despite his great height which is not the ideal qualification for a jumper. With Bali Hai who started her career in Scotland and then showed great form for Mrs. Milner he has established a great partnership, amongst other successes winning the Puissance in Milan. He also has an exceptional horse in El Matador, and on Millstream won the Leipzig Grand Prix (1967).

Jane Kidd achieved her greatest successes at the 1966 Royal International Horse Show, winning two major competitions. Very much a rider who has taken the trouble to profit from the best instruction and example she has become usefully consistent. Consequently she is always reliable as a member of a team, thought big individual wins may elude her.

Our training of show jumpers is not dogmatic but adjusted to the characteristics of our horses. However, it can be divided into three parts—understanding the horse, making him a good ride and developing his jumping ability.

THE TOP TWENTY

Firstly we try to understand the minds of our horses so as to gain their confidence and to develop a temperament which has the cool courage and concentration necessary to take on the big fences. This is best achieved through feeding and type of work. We adjust the feeding so that the horse is fit, feeling well but not scatty. We vary the type of work so that an excitable horse has quiet regular work, a sluggish horse has fast, stimulating work, and a nervous horse is continually introduced to all those things that he finds fearsome.

Our idea of a good ride is a horse that is (1) responsive to hands and legs (2) has rhythm and balance. The former is easiest to achieve when breaking in for it becomes progressively more difficult as the horse becomes set in his ways. Bits can be changed and spurs used, but the best formula is perseverance and patience with continual changes of pace in an enclosed space. Rhythm and balance are developed through long hours of work in a circle. Lunging can help towards this end.

The final part of training is the development of jumping ability. The horse can be taught to use muscles that help him realize his full athletic ability. It is then easier for him to jump from a difficult take-off spot and he need not rely on a brilliant jockey. This can be done through loose school jumping or if this is not possible—jumping on the lunge.

With the rider 'on board' cavalettis are beneficial. We put them in front of a fence at a distance which we vary so that the horse has to take a long stride, a short stride, no stride or two strides. The fence at the end need not be high, but a wide spread is a good way of developing a proper bascule and scope.

Something of the theorist here. It is, of course, this practice of accepted theory allied with a natural ability that has brought the Kidds to the top.

DAVID BOSTON AND WILLIAM BARKER

Two sons of a skilled and dedicated father these young

brothers, David Boston and William Barker achieved the unique distinction of being selected to go to the Tokyo Olympic Games, to represent Britain in show jumping. The elder, David, was in the team, William the reserve.

Under the guidance of their father they produce all their own horses, and their successes have included the 1960 Foxhunter winner Lucky Sam, ridden by Anne, North Riding on which David represented Britain in Germany, Poland, Japan and England and won the 1965 Horse and Hound Cup at the White City, and North Flight the outstanding mare by a Cleveland Bay stallion that twice won for William the National Young Riders Championship and in 1966 the Victor Ludorum at The Horse of the Year Show.

There was always the pony in our family with the natural jumping ability and, as the years have passed, we have become more convinced that only the very rare horse possessing this quality is worthy of having all the time and patience lavished on it necessary for producing a top-grade jumper.

We don't claim any special knowledge of training jumpers —two of our best three horses were brought as young hunters and it was just pure luck that they happened to be natural jumpers. North Flight as an unbroken three-year-old gave no indication of jumping ability until we rode her that winter.

When we are impressed by the performance of a young horse, newly broken (and in most cases they are unbroken or just backed when we get them) we avoid at all costs frightening them by asking them to jump too big. At this stage we feel that patience is vital if we are to build up by degrees a confidence which in time will take them through the hazards of a big competition.

To apply this training to a horse which mentally and physically is unsuited to jumping is likely not only to be a waste of time but amounts in a small degree to cruelty! Horses which obviously jump for fun and make themselves a nuisance by disappearing from the field they should be occupying are usually the best to work on. Lucky Sam, until he was given his donkey companion, was frequently found in the next parish and once escaped over a 6 ft. 7 in. barricade.

Graduating from novice to top-class jumper would appear not to be the result of artificial aids, but purely patience and a high standard of accuracy on the rider's part.

We do not seem able to offer any scientific or technical advice—the hard way through patience and perseverance is the only one we know in pursuing this fascinating but tantalizing sport.

A delightful natural and unsophisticated exposition by two young naturals bears the hallmark of their background: a north-country farm where horses are as much a part of the set-up as the cows—perhaps more: where hunting is the natural winter pastime and schooling ground. All absolutely genuine and very refreshing: and what results it has produced.

DAVID AND VALERIE BARKER

Experts in many countries agree that David Barker is one of the most delightful stylists to watch. His wife, Valerie, is also one of the most competent in the sport, and like her husband a joy to watch. David Barker is, of course, a first cousin of David Boston and William Barker, and so there are four members of one family all of whom have achieved top honours in international jumping.

Both David and Valerie Barker are essentially sympathetic riders: again and again one notices their quietness: and yet they have achieved no less than the toughest and most determined. With Franco David Barker was in our Rome Olympic Team, 1960. On Mr. Softee he won the European Championship in 1962.

Valerie Barker won the richest prize in England when she won the *News of the World* Championship at Ascot in 1964, following it with her win in the Leading Show Jumper of the Year at Wembley. The following year she won two major competitions at Dublin and the Ladies' Championship at Richmond. Before her marriage she was Valerie Clarke who first came into prominence with her ex-hurdler Knight of the Wold, on which she also won many hunter championships, frequently at the same show and on the same day as she won a big show jumping prize.

Most of our horses start their show jumping career in the hunting field. Here they learn good manners, and the solid fences teach them to be sensible and respectful without losing their confidence.

The type of horse most suitable for a show jumper is very controversial, personally we prefer a T.B. or nearly so, around 16 h.h. with a compact body and good strong loins.

The limbs must be as near perfect as possible, as the strain and jar can be tremendous.

Ground work at home is, of course, very important. The horse must learn to mouth properly and accept the bit, so that when the time comes for him to have to turn accurately against the clock his mind will be on the jumps, and not on resisting your pressure on the reins.

You must teach your horse to be flexible and supple on either rein, and when cantering make him extend and shorten his stride with his hocks well under him. Lunging the horse over a small solid pole or parallel bars teaches him to think quickly and helps him find his own stride; keep him on a small circle so that he has to use every muscle. Always wear over-reach boots for this exercise, for it is a pity when a horse puts in extra effort only to be rewarded by a painful over-reach cut.

We like to jump our horses in a snaffle if *possible*, with perhaps a drop nose-band and running martingale, neither of which should be tight. If the horse is too strong in this we prefer a stronger bit rather than to have a pulling battle with him, this way they often learn that to go smoothly is easier for them anyway, and one can then revert back to a plain snaffle. We try to teach our horses to go at an even pace when jumping a course. To have them 'bunched up' in between fences seems unfair to them when sooner or later they will have to travel at 10 m.p.h. faster in order to beat the winning time.

Approach the fence smoothly but on arriving at the fence encourage the horse to put in a shorter stride to take-off on rather than to stand off and have to reach for it. Jumping off a short, collected stride enables him to land in a comfortable and collected manner ready for a fence quickly following or for a quick turn. Be sure to give him plenty of freedom in the air, so that he can use his neck and shoulders to the full.

Once our horses start going to the shows, if all is going well we give them very little jumping at home, perhaps just a pop over a pole six or seven times on a circle the day before to loosen up their muscles.

Try to keep your horse enjoying his job; this way he should be a pleasure to ride and watch.

The above seems to me to have it all: the exactly right mixture practical common sense and expertise. For them there are no gimmicks in training and one can be confident that any horse that comes their way, as long as it has the necessary jump in it, will produce just about all of which it is capable, and on occasions a little bit more.

That they should prefer a thoroughbred is interesting in that Valerie Barker has achieved her greatest successes on Atalanta, a strong active horse, but by no means a thoroughbred. This suggests to me that with the ideal horse Valerie Barker would be almost unbeatable even in the very top class.

This symposium of opinions makes fascinating reading for the student of show jumping, coming as it does in a series of spontaneous and unprompted contributions.

It would seem that there are certain priorities, certain practices, certain qualities, which are virtually common denominators; in particular patience, no schooling over big fences, the importance of the gymnasium—the basic schooling on the ground to make a horse supple and obedient and to strengthen the muscles enabling him to turn quickly and to jump properly.

THE TOP TWENTY

Is there a subtle difference in the contributions from the lady riders, a greater hint of sympathy, perhaps a greater thoroughness? The frequent reference to the value of the use of voice is certainly interesting, and consoling perhaps to less successful riders who may feel that they are being rather soft when talking to their horse or pony.

Brief as their contributions are these top riders have given a most valuable glimpse of behind the scenes, an intriguing insight into the methods employed by those few skilled enough to reach the top in a high complex and demanding sport, and having reached the top to stay there.

The fact that in one country one can find without difficulty as many as twenty top names, all known to the general public, is testimony to the standard of riding in this sport, and our great strength in it. That so obviously others would include names here omitted underlines this.

Indeed, the great difficulty in this chapter has been in selection. Obviously two outstanding young riders, John Ballie and Caroline Bradley, have strong claims for inclusion. But the former has yet to prove himself as more than a one-horse-star—all his major successes have been scored on Dominic: and the outstanding success of the new partnership between the far from easy Franco and the exceptionally promising Caroline Bradley —she won two international competitions at Dublin on her Russian-bred Ivanovitch the first time she represented Britain— happened too late for this book.

Fred Welsh, consistent for so long, merited inclusion, but it was well on in the 1967 season before he really found his old form. The brilliant Mickey Leow hails from South Africa and so perhaps should be regarded as a passing meteor. Doubtless there are others such as Betty Jennaway, winner of the 1967 Queen Elizabeth Cup whom many will consider certainly as good as the names that have been included: possibly better.

I believe, however, that many of their thoughts on the training and schooling of top-class jumpers would have been similar to those recorded.

CHAPTER VIII

Olympic Jumping

The climax of all show jumping with every nation is the Olympic Games. It is not just that it is the most famous sporting event in the world; to win the Olympic jumping is to prove clearly that a nation has the best jumping team. There is never a 'fluke' win in the Olympic Games; this is because the course is that much bigger, that much more demanding, than any other course in the whole of the show-jumping year.

One might say that there are three types of courses. There are the National courses; courses which can be jumped clear by perhaps 10 or 15 per cent of the horses in top-class jumping in that one country. There are the international courses, which can be jumped clear by 10 or 15 per cent from anything between six and fifteen nations taking part. Then there are the Olympic courses, which can be jumped clear by—at the most—2 per cent of the best horses and riders in the world. This gives one some idea of how much bigger an Olympic course is than any other.

A nation, however, knows that it has only so many Olympic-type horses; any nation that is fortunate enough to have three Olympic-type horses realizes that it will have an exceptional chance in the Olympic Games. In all the Olympic Games that I have seen since the War, only once have I seen a nation win the Olympic Games with *three* Olympic-type horses. This, in fact, was the British team at Helsinki in 1952, when the British Team consisted of Foxhunter, Nizefella and Aherlow.

Twice the Germans have had wonderful teams and, in fact, have won the gold medals, but in each case their third horse has been just below Olympic standard.

The majority of nations are well satisfied if they can produce

105

two Olympic horses—the third member of the team being a good international horse. Many teams have to be satisfied with only one Olympic horse, or no Olympic horse at all.

The reason for this is that the Olympic course is not necessarily bigger in that the fences are higher—indeed, they are limited to 5 ft. 3 in.—but the spreads are bigger and, most important of all, the distances between the fences (especially in the combinations) are very demanding. In other words, to get round an Olympic course, a horse must have enormous scope. The ordinary national horse is lucky if it gets round an Olympic course with less than, say, 24 faults and more likely over 30. An international horse is lucky if it gets round an Olympic course with twelve faults or less; that is to say with three fences down. Since the War there have never been more than two clear rounds in an Olympic competition; the average score for a team in an Olympic competition is something between twenty and thirty in each round for the winners—many teams have scores in the fifties and sixties.

An example of this can be seen in the Stockholm Olympic Games in 1956. Germany had obviously two *great* horses, Halla and Meteor; their third horse was a *good* horse—Ala. Halla had 4 faults in the first round and then jumped a clear round in the second round. Meteor had 8 faults in the first round and 4 faults in the second round. Their good horse, Ala, had scores of 16 and 8. Germany won the gold medal with a total of 40.

Italy, too, had two *great* horses and one *good* one. Their great horses, Merano and Uruguay, had scores of 8 and 0 and 8 and 3, respectively. Their good horse did not quite come up to form and had scores of 23 and 24, giving them a total of 66. Great Britain, that year, had but one *great* horse, Nizefella, and he did two great rounds for scores of 8 and 4. The other two horses in their team were *good* horses and jumped good rounds; Flanagan, ridden by Pat Smythe, had 8 and 13, Scorchin, ridden by Peter Robeson, had rounds of 12 and 20—for a total of 69. In fact, Pat Smythe's brilliant riding flattered Flanagan, who performed, thanks to her, very nearly like a great horse, having only eight faults in the first round.

OLYMPIC JUMPING

In the whole of the competition there were only some six other *great* horses competing, no nation having more than one *great* horse in its team. Each of these had a score of between 4 and 20 in one of the two rounds.

From this it will be seen how rare a real Olympic horse is; this, in my opinion, is as it should be, because it means that the right nation wins the Olympic Games. As I have said, there can be no 'fluke' result.

It is possible, therefore, in the Olympic Games to be more or less certain in advance which nations will be concerned with the medals; because one knows how many *great* horses each nation has, and any nation that has two or more *great* horses is bound to be hard to beat; any nation fortunate enough to have three *great* horses is almost certain to win, though admittedly, as has happened on more than one occasion, a *great* horse has jumped below its form so that its team has, as a result, become no more than an ordinary team.

In the Olympic Games each nation is represented by a team of three which jump one after the other—first one from the first team, then one from the second, then one from the third, and so on; the second strings then jump, and finally the third. After an interval there is a second round, and they all jump again. This means that the competition is also a very considerable test of stamina; there is no doubt that one of the reasons Britain won the gold medal at Helsinki in 1952 was because our horses were fitter. The first round had been disappointing for Britain in that one of our three *great* horses, Foxhunter, jumped well below standard and, at the end of the first round, Britain was only in sixth place; but, in the afternoon, when it was extremely hot in that oven-like stadium, the British horses were very much fitter and fresher and did three good rounds, whereas all those nations who had been ahead of us at the end of the first round failed to produce their best form and fell by the wayside. This superior fitness of the British team was due to the fact that, for the first time, a nation had flown its horses—at great expense— to the Olympic Games, and therefore they lost no condition in the usual long journey by sea, rail and road.

OLYMPIC JUMPING

Often people ask one how it is that a certain horse that has been jumping very successfully in national competitions—possibly even in international competitions—can be left out of an Olympic team. The answer is quite simple. That particular horse, brilliant as it may be in national or international competitions, winning frequently in a jump-off against the clock, is not necessarily an Olympic horse, where, although there is a comparatively severe time allowance and a time limit, which makes it very easy to collect time faults, there is no jump-off against the clock, and, therefore, speed is not of any particular merit, nor the ability to jump and turn quickly; it is the scope—the ability to jump big spread fences, the stride enabling a horse to reach easily a second big fence following a previous one only a few strides away—that is important.

Britain has a remarkable Olympic record. In 1948 Britain won the bronze medal, being beaten by Mexico and Spain—two nations which had not been involved in the Second World War that had ended less than three years previously. In 1952 we won the gold medal at Helsinki; in 1956 we won the bronze medal, being beaten, as already described, by Germany and Italy—teams with a higher proportion of *great* horses compared with Britain. In Rome our team was unfortunately eliminated owing to three refusals by Franco, but, in the individual competition, Sunsalve, ridden by David Broome, won the bronze medal. Incidentally, Sunsalve also achieved the most spectacular round of the whole of the competition in the team jumping, achieving, as was then thought, the only clear round, which produced for him a standing ovation from a crowd of 100,000. Later this clear round was amended to four faults, the judge at the water jump having seen a splash which, in fact, was made by some turf being thrown into it by Sunsalve's hooves as they landed as is quite clear in pictures; and it is unfortunate that it robbed Sunsalve of the only clear round of the competition, though it in no way affected the result.

At Tokyo, in 1964, Britain was particularly unfortunate because, earlier in that season, there were no less than six Olympic-type, or *great*, horses from which to choose, putting us in an

108

OLYMPIC JUMPING

almost impregnable position. There were Merely-a-Monarch, Mr. Softee, Harvester, O'Malley, Franco and Firecrest. Unfortunately, however, when the time came for the selectors to choose their team, all but one of these was, for one reason or another, unfit, the team finally consisting of Firecrest, the one Olympic-type horse, Jacapo ridden by David Broome, and North Riding ridden by David Boston Barker. In fact, thanks to courageous performances by the riders, the team managed to come fourth, but there is no doubt that at Tokyo Britain had the best chance of winning a gold medal since Helsinki, twelve years earlier.

At the fifty-ninth minute of the eleventh hour—for show jumping is always the final event of the Olympic Games—Firecrest did in fact win a bronze medal for Britain, having to jump-off against the young Australian rider, John Fahey, on Bonvale, thus maintaining for Britain the remarkable record of winning a medal at every post-war Olympic Games—a record that is unequalled by any other nation.

The problems for our selectors in 1964 spotlight a situation that is likely to recur: certainly it is more likely to with any nation where show jumping is not in any way Government-sponsored. To make ends meet riders have to take their horses to as many shows as they can fit in, picking up as much prize money as they possibly can. They cannot afford to lay-off a horse for three or four weeks in case it gets stale; it is not even easy for them to accept an invitation to jump for Britain on the Continent, entailing their absence from the home shows for two, three or even four weeks. Abroad they will be jumping against very high-class competition and will be lucky if they come home with just two or three third prizes, whereas, if they had stayed at home, they might, in that time, have picked up some £400 or £500 prize money. In addition they are being denied the necessary time to jump and school the horses that they have left behind.

It so happens that the Olympic Games invariably seem to come at the end of the British Show Jumping season; the Rome Olympic Games were in September; the Tokyo Olympic Games

109

were in October, as are the Olympic Games in Mexico. The British show-jumping season starts in April; this means that, by the time the team gets to the Olympic Games, the horses have been jumping for six months. Not surprisingly, they are beginning to tire by this time; they may even be downright stale, and of course, in that six months, there has been plenty of opportunity for horses to fall by the wayside though lameness, foot trouble, heart trouble—all the ailments that assailed us in 1964, in the season before the Olympic Games in Tokyo.

It is difficult to see what the solution to this is. Fortunately, a number of generous patrons, such as Mr. Robert Hanson, Mr. Frank Smith and Mr. Maserella, are now the owners of some of the best horses; and they, of course, can tell their riders that they do not wish the horse, or horses, to jump at so many shows. Usually, however, the rider of a horse owned by one of these generous patrons gets at least 50 per cent of the prize money, so he or she does not really like it if the horse is debarred from jumping at a number of shows at which it would normally jump, and pick up valuable prizes.

However patriotic a young rider may be it is asking an almost superhuman sacrifice if the selectors insist that the horse should be jumped sparingly through the season on the chance that it will be included in the Olympic Games Team. Inclusion cannot ever be considered a certainty, and therefore one might throw away half the season and, at the end of it all, *not* be included in the Olympic team.

Nevertheless, the Olympic Games are the climax of all show jumping and, as in the past, everything possible will always be done to see that Britain does produce the best team with the greatest chance. Britain has always won a medal, but only once a gold medal; there are many people who feel that, with the great successes that British show jumpers are now enjoying in international competition—we virtually won the World Championship in winning the President's Cup in 1965 and 1967—it is time that Britain again won the Olympic Gold Medal.

It has, though, to be remembered that the standard in show jumping the world over is far higher than it was in 1952 when we won at Helsinki. In the countries of many of our strongest opponents show jumping is subsidised, and, therefore, governments are prepared not only to spend large sums of money on training their teams and travelling them all over the Continent, or even the world, gaining international experience; but they also invest huge sums in the buying of top-class international horses: particularly from Britain and Ireland incidentally, which means that British teams are frequently competing against foreign teams composed of British horses.

It is easy enough to understand the temptation for an owner to part with a promising international horse when a foreigner comes along and offers a really big sum. After all, the horse may be lame next week, or lose its nerve.

There is much talk today of the brain drain: there is no less a drain in the world of horses; and it is not only thoroughbreds, but even show jumpers, with the result that Britain is always faced with a big problem in finding Olympic horses.

It is, however, true to say that our leading riders are now bringing into the country horses from overseas, in particular German and South American horses, so perhaps it is beginning to even out.

That I, personally, would like to see a rule whereby nations had to perform on horses bred in their own countries is perhaps beside the point.

CHAPTER IX

Organization

U ndoubtedly one reason for the health and prosperity for the sport of show jumping lies in the fact that it is well organized.

Internationally the official organizing body is the Federation Equestrian Internationale (F.E.I.) which meets regularly under the Presidency of Prince Philip, Duke of Edinburgh, with delegates from all the major countries.

Each country has a federation for its national administration. In Britain it is, of course, the British Show Jumping Association. This body elects a President and a Chairman annually, though, in fact, Colonel Sir Mike Ansell was Chairman for the first twenty years after the war.

It has a Secretary-General, at present Captain G. H. S. Webber, who has also been in office some twenty years.

The Committee consists of eight nationally elected members, in addition to two members nominated by the Scottish branch.

There is no doubt that much of the strength of the B.S.J.A. lies in its regional organization. It may be helpful to set out, as in the B.S.J.A. year book, something of the Regional and Area Organization.

REGIONAL ORGANIZATION

Great Britain is divided into Areas as limited and defined from time to time by the Executive Committee. At present, Areas are usually limited and defined on a County basis, i.e. each County

11. Kick back. Vibart, Andrew Fielder's massive horse with the sledge-hammer kick back. In 1963 and 1966 he won the Leading Jumper of the Year Prize at the Horse of the Year Show, and in 1965 was National Champion.

12a & b. Ever-
greens. Veteran Ted
Williams, doyen of
the show jumpers,
four times Leading
Jumper of the Year
and (*right*) George
Hobbs, three times
second in the King
George V Cup,
Victor Ludorum
at the Horse of the
Year Show, 1964.

forms an Area, but this is not an inflexible policy, and the Executive Committee may from time to time limit and define a new Area and re-limit and re-define any existing Area on any other basis as it thinks fit.

AREA REPRESENTATIVES AND COMMITTEES

The affairs of each Area shall be managed by an Area Committee which shall consist of: (i) the Area Representative; (ii) member or members of the Area who for the time being is or are a Regional or National member or members of the Executive Committee of the Association (hereinafter called 'ex-officio members'); (iii) not less than three or more than nine members of the Area who shall be appointed by the Area Representative and; (iv) such other persons not exceeding three in number as shall be co-opted thereto by the other members of the Area Committee.

If by the 1st day of November in any year one-fifth of the members of an Area entitled to vote at any General Meeting of the Association shall notify the Secretary-General of the Association that it is desired that the appointed members of the Area Committee for the next ensuing year shall be elected by the members of that Area, then the Secretary-General of the Association shall arrange for such an election by postal ballot.

No person shall be qualified to be a member of an Area Committee who is not a member of the Association, or who is an Associate or a Junior Member thereof.

Any general meeting of an Area can be held as, when and where the Area Committee shall appoint and a general meeting of an Area shall be convened by the Area Committee on a request in writing signed by not less than one-fifth of the members of the Area entitled to attend and vote at general meetings of that Area.

No business shall be transacted at any general meeting unless a quorum of members is present at the time when the meeting proceeds to business.

If within half an hour from the time appointed for the meeting a quorum is not present, the meeting shall stand adjourned to the same day in the next week, at the same time and place or to such other place as the Area Committee may by not less than two days' notice to the members of the Area prescribe.

The Area Representative shall be the Chairman of the Area Committee and of general meetings of the Area.

At any general meeting of an Area a resolution put to the vote of the meeting shall be decided on a show of hands unless a poll is (before or on the declaration of the result of the show of hands) demanded:

(*a*) By the Chairman, or

(*b*) By at least three members of the Area present in person and entitled to vote.

A poll demanded on any question shall be taken forthwith.

The only members of an Area entitled to vote at any general meeting of the Area shall be those entitled to vote at any general meeting of the Association.

The duties of each Area Representative and Area Committee are as follows:

(i) To foster within the Area the interests of the Association and to encourage all persons interested in matters appertaining to Show Jumping and Shows holding Jumping Competitions to become Members of the Association.

(ii) To take care of the interests of all Members of the Association within the Area, including the holding of meetings of Junior Members of the Association within the Area at which their parents may attend, if it is considered that such a meeting or meetings is required.

(iii) To ensure the attendance of the Area Representative or of a member of the Area Committee at every Affiliated Show in the Area at which Jumping Competitions are or are likely to be held. The person attending should make himself known to the Secretary of the Show and, if requested to do so, should render assistance in the preliminary lay-out of the Jumping Course and co-operate with the Executive of the Show and the Judges in ensuring the smooth running of the Jumping Competitions.

(iv) To ensure that any infringement of the Rules or Regulations of the Association is reported to the Secretary-General of the Association.

(v) To advise the Secretary-General of the Association of the names of all members for the time being of the Area Committee, and to send him a copy of the Minutes of every meeting of the Area Committee and of every general meeting of the Area.

Each Area Committee shall hold at least one meeting in each year and if only one such meeting is held in any year such meetings shall be held not earlier than sixty days or later than three days prior to the Area and Branch Representatives' Meeting to be held by the Association in that year.

If the Area Representative or, where existent, Area Committees of two or more adjoining Areas shall consider it desirable to form a Branch, then notification to that effect shall be sent to the Secretary-General of the Association, together with details of the Area concerned. The matter will then be placed before the Executive Committee, who, if they consider it desirable that a Branch shall be formed, may authorize the formation thereof.

The duties of each Branch are as follows:

(i) To foster within the Branch District (hereinafter defined) the interests of the Association and to encourage all persons interested in matters appertaining to Show Jumping and Shows holding jumping competitions, to become Members of the Association.

(ii) To take care of the interests of all Members of the Association within the Branch District.

(iii) To ensure the attendance of a member of the Committee of Management at every Affiliated Show in the Branch District at which jumping competitions are or are likely to be held. The person attending should make himself known to the Secretary of the Show and, if requested to do so, should render assistance in the preliminary lay-out of the Jumping Course and co-operate with the Executive of the Show and the Judges in ensuring the smooth running of the jumping competitions.

(iv) To ensure that any infringement of the Rules or Regulations of the Association is reported to the Secretary-General of the Association.

ORGANIZATION

(v) To ensure the attendance of a member of the Committee of Management at the Area and Branch Representatives' Meeting, which will be held by the Association once in each year immediately prior to the Annual General Meeting of the Association. (Neither the Area Representative of any Area included in a Branch nor a member of the Committee of any such Area is required to attend the Area and Branch Representatives'Meeting).

The membership subscription for a jumping member is £3 p.a. Non-jumping members pay £1 and juniors (jumping) £1 10s. 0d. In addition visitors from other countries can become members for £3 p.a. A service unit or a saddle club can become a corporate member for £5 p.a.

Members of the B.S.J.A. can only compete at shows which are affiliated to the Association. The fee for affiliation is £3 10s. 0d. and carries valuable insurance cover against Third Party and Public Liability risks.

A further means of producing the necessary income to administer the association efficiently is the levy on prize money. Any exhibitor winning more than £100 in any one year is levied at the rate of $2\frac{1}{2}$ per cent. It is also suggested that affiiliated shows should contribute to the Olympic Games and Equestrian Fund which finds the money to send teams overseas. This contribution is worked out at 6d. in the pound of the total prize money.

To ensure that the prize money is properly distributed it is laid down that the first prize should never be more than one-third of the total prize, so that it is possibly to offer prizes to those well down the line, in order that as many people as possible may find it worth their while to compete.

It is further laid down that there must be a prize for every five starters, the lowest prize never being less than the entry fee.

As has already been made clear, course building is an art. The B.S.J.A., therefore, has a panel of Voluntary Course Builders—there are nearly a hundred of them—who are available to help those shows unable to afford the official professional course builders employed by the B.S.J.A.

The B.S.J.A. also has sets of show jumps which affiliated shows may hire.

ORGANIZATION

Finally the Association offers valuable help in the actual organization of the show, and again it may be useful to quote from their handbook.

RUNNING THE SHOW TO TIME

Show Executives are urged to read this paragraph, as it is probably the most important in this pamphlet.

To be a success, a Show must run approximately to time, a Show which runs late, not only gives itself a bad name, but also affects other Shows, and brings the sport in general into disrepute. The following is suggested for consideration by Show Executives:

(*a*) Schedule—When drawing up the schedule, it should be remembered that on an average a jumping round takes $2\frac{1}{2}$ minutes, it is, therefore, no good to include several Jumping Classes and to receive unlimited entries for each Class. Therefore, decide on a suitable number of competitions that may be held in the time available, and then consider how these entries may be controlled:

(i) State in the schedule that only . . . entries will be accepted in this Class.

(ii) If two competitions are held, do not allow the same horses to compete in both.

(iii) Include a general clause that if necessary a 'standard' may be introduced by the Judges.

(*b*) Closing dates of entries.

A closing date for entries must be fixed, this should be sufficiently in advance of the Show to enable an accurate time-table to be produced and for a catalogue to be printed.

(*c*) Final Planning of the Time-Table

An approximate time-table should always be included in the schedule, as exhibitors will want to know whether they have to travel overnight, in order to be in the ring very early, or whether they may go to another Show first.

When all the entries have been received a detailed time-table

117

should be produced, and sent to all competitors. If large entries have been received, the Secretary must do something immediately, it is no good hoping a miracle will happen on Show day. He may:

(i) If sufficient room is available, erect another ring where some classes may be judged.

(ii) Start earlier, but be sure to give exhibitors plenty of warning about this, it is better to start earlier than have chaos and have to cancel classes at the end of the day.

(iii) Instruct the Judge to bring in a standard as soon as possible. Unless it is absolutely essential, do not do this in Foxhunter and Grade 'C' Competitions.

(*d*) The day of the Show

The organizer, having planned his final time-table, will have discussed it with his senior stewards. He will have stressed the 'danger spots' where the Show may get behind time, and all will be on their guard against this.

During a jumping class, the senior steward should be watching the time throughout. The first ten horses have taken 25 minutes, we must do better than that. Can we get the horses in more quickly? Could we bring the next one in on this side of the arena before the previous one finishes?

As the class progresses, he realizes that a 'standard' must be brought in if the class is not to run very late and he discusses this with the Judges. An announcement is then made, explaining the position.

Towards the end of the class, he warns the collecting ring steward of the probable result and tells him to get the riders ready to come in either for a jump-off, or for the awards. Surely, the V.I.P. who is to give the cup, will only want to make the presentation to the winner, and a judge or steward could give out the other awards; every minute counts.

Throughout the day every minute saved counts, and it has been known for 25 minutes to be taken over the awards. How boring for the spectators on the other side of the ring, or at the end of the arena!

If the senior steward is really active and conscious of the

importance of time, it is unbelievable how many precious seconds can be saved. In a class of sixty competitors, 10 seconds saved on each amounts to 10 minutes.

SHOW GROUND ORGANIZATION

GENERAL

Show Executives are reminded of their responsibility to take adequate precautions for the safety of the public at their Show. The Show Ring should be enclosed either by fencing or a stout rope with stakes at frequent intervals and on no account should the public be allowed inside the ring.

Sufficient Stewards and/or Police Officers should be available to ensure that the public are kept to the proper side of the fence and it is advisable to warn the public from time to time over the loud-speaker system, that they must not encroach within the area roped off, and that if they do, it will be at their own risk.

It is a further responsibility of the Show Executive to ensure that the entrance and exit of the Main Ring is kept clear of spectators and sufficient Stewards and/or Police Officers must be made available for this purpose.

Where tip-ups for animals are provided and it is desired to set aside a portion of the ground for this purpose, the division should be made with either a rope and posts or suitable fences. On no account should barbed wire be used, as this constitutes a danger to animals, which would almost certainly be regarded as negligence on the part of a Show in the event of an accident.

Show Executives are particularly reminded of the 'Keep Britain Tidy' campaign, and it is the responsibility of the Show Executives to provide the necessary receptacles for litter and also for empty bottles, whether whole or broken, as they are a constant danger to horses and other livestock. An accident due to a broken bottle would probably be regarded as negligence on the part of the Show. Announcements should be made at various times throughout the day asking the public to use the receptacles provided for their rubbish, thus ensuring that the Showground is left clean and tidy at the end of the day.

ORGANIZATION

Make adequate provisions for Exhibitors to be able to watch their horses jumping by allotting them a small reserved enclosure, and also help them by arranging free car parking as near to the horse lines or Collecting Ring as possible.

Long Jumping Classes are apt to become tedious to the public, and it is better to divide a big Class by bringing on some other attraction in the middle, rather than to have continuous jumping for a long period. When this is done, competitors must be informed in advance in which part of the Competition they will be required to jump.

If a time-table is published, every effort must be made to keep to it, as Competitors from long distances have grounds for complaint if they are kept waiting long after the advertised time of the competition.

Show Executives are strongly advised to stage their Jumping competitions well before the end of the programme. Many people come especially to see the Jumping and are very disappointed if they miss it, or have to stay late in order to see it. At a one-day Show the Open Junior and Open Adult Competition should have been completed by 6 p.m.

PRACTICE JUMPS

Show Executives are reminded of the importance of providing adequate and safe arrangements for Jumping Competitors to warm up and limber up their animals before competing. If space allows, a separate Exercise Area, not too far from the Collecting Ring, should be provided and two Practice Jumps, one straight and one spread, available. If these are able to be arranged in 'lanes', one jumped one way and the other jumped coming back, it is much less dangerous and overcrowding is reduced to a minimum.

STEWARDS

It is impossible for a Show Organizer to run a Show efficiently without enough Stewards, and these should be selected well before the Show and well briefed as to their particular duties. The following will be found necessary for Jumping Competitions:

Chief Ring Steward. His duty is to ensure that the Show runs to time and he is the most important Steward. He should also be present when the course is built and control the Arena Party.

Accident Drill. A veterinary surgeon should always be in attendance in case of an accident, and the procedure should be agreed with him how an accident or injury to a horse in the ring may be dealth with. A canvas screen should be available in the event of an accident, and the Arena Party should be rehearsed in the procedure to be adopted if it should be wanted.

Arena Party or Jump Stewards. These Stewards will be controlled by the Chief Ring Steward but will work under the Course Builder. They should have an N.C.O. or foreman in charge of them. If possible a military arena party is best to have; however, if they are not available, there are plenty of local organizations, such as Scouts or Young Farmers, who would probably be only too willing to assist. They should not have any other duties to perform at the Show, and should always be present when the course is being built, so that the Course Builder may brief them and they may become familiar with the fences.

A *Judges' Steward* should always be available to assist the Judges and produce the rosettes at the end of a competition, so that there is no delay. He should also ensure that the results are sent immediately to the Awards Office.

Collecting Ring Steward. Much of the success of the Show will depend on how quickly the horses are sent into the Ring. Therefore, the Collecting Ring Steward should draw up an order of jumping well in advance of the competition starting, so that competitors may know when they are due in the Ring. When an order of jumping is drawn by ballot, this must be strictly adhered to. It is always drawn when the jump-off is on time.

The order of jumping should be displayed on a blackboard and should be raised sufficiently high enough from the ground to enable the competitor to read it from his horse. A notice should be displayed by the side of it to the effect that any competitor missing his turn may be eliminated.

COMMUNICATIONS

If telephone communications are installed, these should operate between the Judges, the Collecting Ring, the Secretary's Office and the Commentator, if he is not with the Judges.

When possible the Commentator should always be with the Judges and as much use made of the Public Address Equipment as possible.

The Commentator, who should be a person with some knowledge of the horses and riders, will be able to increase the interest for the public very considerably.

He should always refrain from commentating while a competitor is actually jumping.

The horse-box and stable area should always be covered by the loud-speaker system, so that competitors may be called for and know what is happening in the ring.

A well-run show gives the impression of everything happening easily, automatically and efficiently. In fact a great deal of careful organization is necessary if the show is going to run in such a way that it satisfies the exhibitors and entertains the public.

CHAPTER X

The Rules

For a long time there was very considerable variation between the F.E.I. (international) and B.S.J.A. (national) rules. But they are now virtually the same.

All competitions are judged in accordance with the Regulations and Rules of the F.E.I. or B.S.J.A.

The horses are judged solely on their performance over the obstacles, and although the element of time enters into the judging of some competitions, the style of the horse and rider is not considered: hence the spectator can easily understand the rules.

THE COURSES AND THE OBSTACLES

The courses with the obstacles are carefully planned to provide certain tests for horse and rider. These courses will not only provide a test of obedience and speed. The well-trained, supple, and obedient horse will gain the advantage over the untrained horse.

The obstacles will vary in nature, some requiring the horse to spread himself as in the case of a triple bar, and others will merely test the horse in his ability to jump a great height as in the case of a straight wall or gate. Fences will usually vary between 4 ft 3 in. and 5 ft. high, and any fence exceeding 5 ft. may be classed as very large. The World's High Jump Record is 8 ft. $0\frac{1}{4}$ in. but this was over a single obstacle with the horse being permitted three attempts. The obstacles should be solid in appearance: the poles used at most shows weigh between 45 lb. and 70 lb. These poles are held in cups.

The spectator studying the lay-out will notice that the fences requiring the horse to spread are interspaced with straight or perpendicular fences. It will also be noticed that there are combinations of fences known as Doubles, or Trebles, which allow the horse only a few strides between the fences. The distances between these vary and so provide another test of obedience for the horse.

The spectator will derive much interest from studying the course and watching how the various riders approach and jump the variety of obstacles.

METHOD OF JUDGING—INTERNATIONAL RULES

There are three categories under which the competitions may be judged—Tables A, B and C.

TABLE A

First disobedience	3 faults
Obstacle knocked down	4 faults
Flag knocked down, or both obstacle and flag knocked down	4 faults
Second disobedience	6 faults

(Faults for disobedience are cumulative, not only at the same obstacle, but throughout the same round).

Fall of horse, or rider, or both   8 faults

(Faults for the fall are in addition to any other faults incurred at the same time).

Third disobedience   Elimination

Exceeding the Time Allowed—for each commenced second $\frac{1}{4}$ fault

(The Time Allowed is calculated from the length of the course and the speed laid down for the competition).

In this Table A the element of Time does not enter into

awards except in the case of equality, in which case Time may decide at the first round or at a subsequent round. This is stated in the programme in the conditions of the competition, and in this round, should any horses be equal in faults, the horse which has completed the round in the fastest time is the winner.

TABLE B

This competition is a test not only for jumping capabilities but also a test of speed and obedience.

For each knock down or foot in the water the competitor is penalized 10 seconds. Falls and the first two disobediences are penalized by the extra time taken, but the third disobedience entails elimination.. The competitor who completes the course in the fastest time with the penalty points added is the winner.

TABLE C

For each obstacle, or flag, knocked down the competitor is penalized a number of seconds between 3 and 17, the actual penalty being calculated according to the length of the course and the number of obstacles.

Falls and the first disobediences are not penalized except by the extra time taken by the competitor, but a third disobedience or any of the occurrences listed below entail elimination.

The competitor who completes the course in the fastest time with the penalty points added is the winner.

Courses for these competitions are usually twisty and have sharp turns. The fast horse who is obedient may beat the slow careful horse, even though the former may have knocked down one or two obstacles.

METHOD OF JUDGING—NATIONAL RULES
(B.S.J.A.)

These are the same as the International Rules—Table A.

THE RULES

METHOD OF TIMING

The competitor on starting his round, breaks a ray thus starting an electric clock in the judge's box. On finishing he again breaks a ray this time stopping the clock.

Competitors may be divided by 1/10th of a second, should the division be less the competitors will be placed as equal.

Should a competitor refuse and in doing so knock down the fence, he must place himself in a position ready to start. The time is then taken off whilst the fence is rebuilt. The time is never taken off when the competitor falls.

ELIMINATION

In all jumping competitions the rider is eliminated for the following occurrences:

(a) Failure to be ready to enter the arena when called.

(b) Jumping any obstacle in the arena, before the starting signal, even if it is not included in the course.

(c) Crossing the starting line before the starting signal is given.

(d) Failing to cross the starting line within 60 seconds of the starting signal.

(e) Third disobedience in the whole round.

(f) Showing any obstacle to the horse before starting, or after a refusal.

(g) Entering or leaving the ring dismounted without special permission of the President of the Ground Jury.

(h) Resistance of the horse during the round at any one time exceeding 60 seconds.

(i) Taking more than 60 seconds to jump an obstacle (except in the case of a fall).

(j) Jumping an obstacle without having rectified a deviation from the course.

(k) Jumping an obstacle not forming part of the course.

(l) Jumping an obstacle in the wrong order.

126

THE RULES

(*m*) Passing the wrong side of a flag, if not rectified.

(*n*) Exceeding the Time Limit. (Twice the Time Allowed.)

(*o*) Jumping an obstacle which has been kncoked down, before it has been re-set.

(*p*) Starting again after an interruption, before the signal to continue has been given.

(*q*) After a disobedience or fall at a double, treble or multiple obstacle failing to re-start jumping over the whole of the (except for a completely closed obstacle).

(*r*) Failure to jump each fence of a double, treble or multiple obstacle, separately.

(*s*) Failure to cross the finishing line mounted, before leaving the arena.

(*t*) The rider and/or horse leaving the arena before the completion of the round.

(*u*) Receiving unauthorized assistance, whether solicited or not, at the discretion of the Ground Jury.

(*v*) Failing to have the required minimum weight when weighing in after completion of the round.

(*w*) Entering the arena on foot after the start of the competition, at the discretion of the Ground Jury.

(*x*) Failing to comply with the conditions of a competition stipulating that part of the course is to be ridden at a trot or a walk.

(*y*) Jumping an optional obstacle more than once in a jump-off.

The actual B.S.J.A. rules enlarge on some of these points as follows:

STARTING AND FINISHING

(*a*) Except for penalties under special Rules competitors are only liable to faults whilst between the starting and finishing posts.

(*b*) Competitors must enter and leave the ring mounted. Entering or leaving the ring dismounted without special permission from the Judge(s) incurs elimination.

THE RULES

(*c*) Competitors may be led into the ring, but the leader must leave the Ring directly the horse/pony is inside.

(*d*) If a Competitor fails to enter the ring within one minute of being called upon to do so he/she will be eliminated.

(*e*) When a Competitor enters the Ring, he/she is under the orders of the Judge(s), but must not start until instructed to do so by the Judge(s). Starting before being instructed to do so will incur elimination.

(*f*) Competitors must start as soon as they are called upon to do so by the Judge(s) and any Competitor who has not passed through the Starting Flags within one minute of having received the signal from the Judge(s) will be eliminated.

Note. Competitors can do much towards helping the Show to keep to time by starting at once.

(*g*) Competitors must always go through the Starting and Finishing Flags or Posts mounted in the direction indicated on the Course plan or by the Judge(s) instructions. Failure to do so incurs elimination.

SHOWING AN OBSTACLE

The action of showing an obstacle to the Horse/Pony before the start or after a refusal, and before resuming the course, is penalized by elimination.

JUMPING THE WRONG COURSE

Should a Competitor jump, or attempt to jump, an obstacle in the wrong order or miss out an obstacle and jump or attempt to jump the next, he/she will be eliminated. But if the Competitor after missing an obstacle returns to the correct obstacle before he/she jumps or attempts to jump another it will be faulted as for a refusal. If an unbroken track is marked on the Course Plan it must be followed.

13. Chief Barker. C. David Barker, a member of the 1960 Olympic team and European Champion in 1962.

14. Mrs. Barker, winner of the Grand Prix at her first international show, Rotterdam, in 1960. In 1964 she was Leading Jumper of the Year.

15. Barker ma: David Boston Barker, a member of the British Olympic team at Tokyo in 1964 on North Riding.

16. Barker mi: William Barker, reserve at Tokyo on North Flight, Victor Ludorum at the Horse of the Year Show, 1965.

THE RULES

LEAVING THE RING

Any Horse/Pony/Rider that leaves the Ring after having come under the orders of the Judge(s) and before completing its round shall be eliminated whatever the manner of their exit.

DIVISION OF PRIZES AND JUMPING-OFF

A jump-off only takes place to decide between those tying for first place.

It is the duty of the Judge(s) to try to obtain a Winner of every Competition and he should set his Courses with that end in view.

In all Jumping Competitions, with the exception of Test Competitions, not more than two Jumps-off will be held.

In the event of a Competitor or Competitors, who have been instructed to Jump-off, declining to do so, the Judge(s) shall disqualify him/them unless the appeal not to jump again is supported by Medical or Veterinary opinion.

A rider will never be required to jump-off against himself when he is riding all the Horses in the Jump-off.

Horses belonging to the same owner will never be required to jump-off against each other if they are the only horses in the Jump-off.

If time may be the deciding factor in the Jump-off, the order of jumping shall be determined by a draw irrespective of whether the original order for the Competition has been drawn or not. The arrangements for the draw shall be the responsibility of the Judge(s).

REFUSALS, ETC.

A circle, turn round, run out or resistance counts as a refusal for scoring purposes.

THE RULES

Definition of a resistance. If a Horse/Pony, wherever he may be, refuses to go forward, stops, runs back, rears, etc., it shall be deemed a resistance. If an unruly Horse/Pony continues to resist and takes longer than one minute to jump an obstacle it shall be eliminated.

A refusal consists of stopping in front of or passing an obstacle to be jumped whether or not the Horse/Pony knocks it down or displaces it. If there is any displacement or any adjustment necessary to the obstacle, the Judge will signal the Competitor to stop and he/she must not re-take the obstacle until a further signal is given by the Judge. When the obstacle has been re-set the Judge will signal and the clock will be re-started. A Competitor who jumps or attempts to jump an obstacle before the signal to re-start will be eliminated.

Stopping at an obstacle without resistance, without knocking it down and without reining back followed immediately by a standing jump is not penalized. If the halt is sustained or if the Horse/Pony reins back even for a single pace, voluntarily or not, a refusal is incurred.

If a Horse/Pony refuses and slides through the obstacle the Competitor must return and await the re-setting of the obstacle and then re-jump it.

If a Horse/Pony having knocked down an obstacle in stopping or slipping, jumps the obstacle before it has been re-erected, he is eliminated.

After being eliminated for refusing, a Competitor may make up to two attempts to jump any other obstacle in the Arena before leaving.

Refusal at a Combination Obstacle (Double or Treble): Clearing an obstacle which is a Double or Treble constitutes a particular test and the obstacles cannot, therefore, be separated. When an obstacle composed of more than one element is to be taken in two or more leaps by the Horse/Pony, the faults at each will be marked separately. Consequently, the refusal, run-out or fall in between any of these obstacles necessitates the rider starting over again from the first of these obstacles. A refusal due to a fall in between any of these obstacles is not penalized.

130

THE RULES

FALL

A Horse/Pony is considered to have fallen when the shoulder and quarters on the same side touch the ground or touch the obstacle and ground.

A rider is considered to have fallen when there is separation between him and his horse which necessitates his remounting or vaulting into the saddle.

Basically the rules are extremely simple and, as has already been suggested, in the vast majority of cases the spectator is quite capable of judging for himself.

On the other hand, as in any sport, there are technicalities and those who want to be closely associated with or identified with the sport should of necessity be conversant with these technicalities. There is always the odd if isolated occasion when a result or decision hinges on the interpretation of a technicality. The good judge, the experienced rider, or the informed spectator knows at once the proper interpretation and decision.

By and large the detail of the rules in show jumping is for the benefit of the competitor. On the other hand show jumping is a spectator sport and not only the rules but the whole planning and consideration of a show jumping competition is planned with this in mind: hence the basic simplicity, the overall straight-forward approach to the sport.

Any spectator will derive increased interest in the sport if conversant with the rules which are, if one thinks about it, the basic prop of any successful and popular sport.

CHAPTER XI

Accusations of Cruelty

Most people interested in show-jumping will have hea rumours from time to time of alleged cruelty in t training of show jumpers even by the top riders. Su allegations appeared in a newspaper article shortly before t Horse of the Year Show—the climax of the show jumpi season—in 1966.

These accusations inevitably did the sport a certain amount harm, because many people took them seriously. They al caused the riders themselves considerable resentment, becau probably there are no greater horse-lovers than those who a the top of the various equestrian sports, including show jum ing.

It would, however, be idle to pretend that, in a sport whi has a membership of over 8,000, of which nearly thre quarters participate, there is no cruelty whatever. Inevitab there are black sheep in any sporting community—and sho jumping is no exception. I will not even pretend that there a not incidents from time to time even amongst those at the tc but I am equally convinced that they are few and far betwee and even more convinced that, in the stewards of the Briti Show Jumping Association, there exists a body of vigilant, e perienced men of complete integrity, who are as anxious as t most soft and sympathetic spectator that there should be t very minimum of cruelty.

That the stewards are backed up by the regulations is obvic from various British Show Jumping Association rules that see to me to be worth quoting: in particular:

132

ACCUSATIONS OF CRUELTY

Rule 5 (b) 'No member shall conduct himself in a manner which, in the opinion of the disciplinary authority, is detrimental to the character and/or prejudicial to the interests of the Association and/or show jumping.'

This seems to me to sum up the whole attitude of the B.S.J.A. Nothing must be allowed to happen, or to be seen to happen, that is prejudicial to the good name and the good reputation of the sport.

But in fact, other rules are far more specific. :

Rule 5 (a): 'No Member shall

(ii) 'ill-treat in any way a horse/pony at a show, whether inside or outside the ring.

(iii) 'Misuse a whip or spur, or carry or use whilst riding a horse/pony in the ring, the collecting ring, or anywhere on or in the immediate vicinity of the show ground, a whip exceeding 30 inches in overall length.

(iv) 'Rap a horse/pony, NOR jump a rail or obstacle which is held by hand and not supported by a stand in the collecting ring or anywhere on or in the immediate vicinity of the show ground.

(v) 'Administer any stimulant or depressant to a horse/pony or cause one to be administered in any way whatsoever, either during any competition or within a period of 48 hours from the start of a competition.

(vi) 'Conduct himself at a show in a manner which is offensive to the public'.

This last, of course, implies excessive punishment of a horse, for this inevitably offends the spectators.

Later in the rules there is a clause to the effect that no substiture for a whip may be carried in any jumping competition and a further clause on martingales. This precludes the use of an excessively tight martingale, adding:

'the only rein permitted is one which runs from the rider's hands direct to the bit ring or to the caveson, in the case of a bitless bridle. Gag reins or check reins of any description are not permitted.'

The rules further stipulate that no item of saddlery or equipment may be misused—a point that I will refer to a little later on.

It goes without saying that the officials of a show insist that any horse at the show may be submitted to a veterinary examination if it is thought necessary.

The penalties for infringements are heavy. The stewards have at all times power to consider the conduct of a member and then, if, in their opinion, the member has been found guilty, they can direct:

(1) that any such member shall be suspended from all or any of the rights and privileges of the membership, for a period, initially, not exceeding twelve months;

(2) that a member shall pay a fine not exceeding £100;

(3) that such a member, whether continuing as a member or not, shall be debarred, for such period as they shall determine, from entering any horse or pony for jumping competition.

In effect, a member found guilty of cruelty can be barred from jumping for life.

There are further safeguards not generally known to the general public; these concern the height of fences. Except in a jump-off, Grade 'C' fences are limited to 4 ft. 3 in.; ponies—4 ft. 3 in., and smaller ponies 3 ft. 9 in. Grade 'B' fences are limited to 4 ft. 6 in.

Furthermore, when the height of a fence is 4 ft., the spread must not exceed 4 ft.; when the height of the fence is 3 ft. 9 in. the spread must not exceed 3 ft. 6 in. In the case of a triple bar—as I have said in an earlier chapter, possibly the easiest fence of all—the overall spread can be as much as 5 ft.

It is carefully laid down what the distances between the elements of a combination fence—a double or treble—should be, to ensure that the fence does not, in any way, become a trap.

Every year the stewards of the B.S.J.A. interview and, in certain cases, suspend, riders who have been reported for adopting cruel methods in the schooling of their horses; most of these, of course, take place on the show ground itself, behind the horse boxes, at the back of the field, or somewhere tucked away in a corner behind a big tent. It is comparatively easy to detect these infringements when they occur; it is not, of course, so easy to detect cruelty in the training methods employed at the rider's home.

There is no doubt that certain riders may use particularly severe methods—perhaps the commonest is what is known as 'rapping': a bar, fixed at one end, held by hand at the other and lifted just as the horse jumps, so that he gets a sharp rap either on his shins or on his hind legs, which has the effect of making him think 'That's funny. I thought I was jumping high enough, but I must have misjudged it. Next time I will jump a little bit higher'. Although this is not a particularly attractive way of making a horse pick up his feet, the cruelty here is of a minimum and can, in fact, be totally non-existent. But there are, of course, crueller methods, such as 'rapping' with an iron bar—a bar with tintacks in, and so on.

There was even an electric gadget fixed to a saddle by some clown, so that when he pressed with his knees the horse got an electric shock! Such extreme practices are, of course, rare in the extreme.

How much are unethical methods employed?

The situation was probably summed up by the well-known rider who once said to me, 'The quickest way of reducing the value of a good horse from £5,000 to £50 is to indulge in cruel training practices, because, although the short-term results may be satisfactory in teaching a horse to be more careful through physical fear, nevertheless the long-term results are bound to be disastrous because very quickly the horse will go sour and refuse to jump at all.'

It seems obvious to me, then, that it just is not worth a rider's while to be cruel in his training methods. In the first place, he risks being 'warned off' and thus, if not losing his livelihood, at least forgoing all his pleasure and enjoyment associated with show jumping. Secondly, he risks reducing the value of his horse.

This is an important point. The value of the horse is virtually the only reward in show jumping; once a horse has been up-graded—that is to say, when he has won £200 or more—then the value of the horse increases very considerably. It can, in fact, be worth anything between £1,000 and £25,000. The owners of a show jumper, by selling good horses that have been up-graded, can make a lot of money, They can never make a lot of money out of winning prizes. In 1966 only fifteen people won more than £1,000; this would barely cover the cost of travelling two or three horses all round the shows during a jumping season; the cost of labour, forage, petrol, transport generally, and occasionally accommodation being so high. It is essential, therefore, if a show jumper is going to keep in the game (unless he has considerable private means) that he must be able to sell, from time to time, an up-graded horse at a big profit—probably overseas. He will, therefore, want to do nothing that is likely to reduce the value of that horse. Moreover, the higher his reputation, as a horsemaster, stands in international circles, the more likely people are to want to buy his horses, because it will be known that they have been properly trained, and schooled, well looked after and well treated.

One must, however, be realistic about the punishment of horses; so often people approach this problem—especially if they have had little to do, themselves, with horses—from a sentimental angle. While nobody wants to hurt a horse unnecessarily, it would be ridiculous to pretend that a horse should never be punished. A horse weighs half a ton, has great strength, is capable of great speeds. Unless it is absolutely obedient, it can be dangerous. This is the basic reason and justification for proper schooling of a horse or pony. But, when it comes to show jumping, the problem becomes more acute. The standard today is so high that one error can cost a rider a big prize, a big increase in the value of the horse, and his reputation as a top-class rider.

It is absolutely essential, therefore, that a horse must learn to jump accurately, as it must learn to be balanced and steady and controlled.

Like human beings, horses can easily become careless or casual; once this happens, then they pick up faults unnecessarily. Obviously from time to time, for one reason or another, a horse will meet a fence so wrongly that it is bound to fault at it; but nothing is more annoying for the rider when having got his horse exactly rightly placed for a perfect take-off, then carelessly the horse just trails a hind leg or fails to lift his knees sufficiently high, and a pole rolls off for 4 faults. This careless effort can cost the rider a place in the jump-off and perhaps a prize of anything up to £750; to say nothing of a place in a representative team. In many instances careful schooling will rectify a horse's carelessness, or a rider may discover that that horse is, for one reason or another, off colour; but particularly with young horses, before they have fully appreciated what is expected of them, these careless tendencies will develop. It is absolutely essential for them to be corrected.

Apart from the use of the voice and perhaps a rather violent correction through the hands, there is no alternative to a sharp smack; possibly a good hiding. A horse that has a streak of obstinacy or laziness in him has, sooner or later, to be taught a lesson. It is not possible, unfortunately, to reason with a horse, to argue the matter out, to explain the situation, as it is with a child; though there are still many people who believe that, with a recalcitrant, obstinate or lazy child, a sharp smack delivered in the right place at the right time is more effective than a lot of arguing and reasoning. Be that as it may, it is not possible to reason with a horse, which leaves one only with the physical correction.

A horse has an extremely thick hide and, although a hit with a stick may sound or even look very vicious, it is in all probability only hurting the horse very slightly and, certainly in no lasting manner.

Unless a fault of laziness or obstinacy is corrected, then the value of that horse is being reduced daily. It is obvious, therefore, that the owner or rider of a horse with a real potential is going to do everything in his power to see that that potential is realized—indeed, he cannot afford to do otherwise.

This proper correction of a fault is not limited to jumping; one cannot help feeling that it is a pity that more people do not more often take the trouble to correct a horse's faults, in the early stages. Take kicking for example. A horse or pony which kicks is not only a menace to anyone who goes riding with that horse or pony—or, indeed, who is near to it at all when it is in a vicious mood—but that kick can, quite easily, be positively dangerous, even lethal. If the horse or pony who finds that he can get away with kicking is properly corrected in the early stages, then he will give it up. I cannot see that this proper correction can be labelled cruelty; yet, again and again, one hears ignorant people accusing a rider of cruelty because he has hit his horse in the ring, trying to teach it a lesson, either to ensure its being safe, or to ensure its reaching its maximum potential, and therefore value as a show jumper.

The following may be somewhat irrelevant, but I think it helps to make my point:

At a pony Club Meet of the hounds of which I am Master a pony viciously kicked out and lamed another pony. The little girl riding the kicker did nothing. I told her to hit her horse really hard; she failed to do so. I told her to get off and I myself gave the pony a really good hiding. The little girl remounted, in tears, and went home. Two days later I had an infuriated letter from the girl's parent, saying that, in the first place, I had no right to hit somebody else's pony—which I cannot really deny: in the second place, I had shown myself capable of excessive cruelty, with which, of course, I did not agree. Three years later, when the little girl was more or less grown up, she came up to me out hunting and said, 'I feel I must tell you that, from the day you hit my pony, it never kicked again. Up till that time it had made my life a misery because it kicked out at everything in sight. Not only', she added, 'did you teach the pony a lesson, but you taught me one which I have never forgotten'.

I am not, of course, advocating excessive punishment—let alone cruelty. I am, however, justifying proper correction of a horse if it is being allowed to get into careless habits which can diminish its value. Show jumping today is big business, in that horses change hands at tremendous prices; were it not for these big prices there would be no show jumping at all, for, as I have said, there is no money to be made out of prizes. It is, therefore, imperative that horses jump accurately and to the very height of their ability; to see that they do this will not only demand extremely thorough and painstaking training—it will also entail *firmness*; but this in no way implies cruelty, and if, occasionally, there are offenders who go beyond the limits of firmness, then, nine times out of ten, they are apprehended by the stewards and penalized—penalized severely.

The vast majority of horses seen show jumping by the general public really love their jumping; they certainly would not do so if they had experienced cruelty in their initial training and schooling.

CHAPTER XII

Reasons for the Popularity of Show Jumping

That show jumping today is a popular spectator sport cannot be denied. It should not be thought, however, that it is only popular in our own times, for it had, in fact, a considerable popularity pre-war, though of course its popularity was rather more exclusive. The show-jumping at the old International Horse Show at Olympia, at the big shows near London—such as Richmond—was extremely popular with large audiences, but in those days far more people were closely connected with horses than in the years immediately after the war, when show jumping was reborn. Nevertheless there were real stars such as Tommy Glencross, the Taylor brothers and Miss Bullows.

There was, of course, no television then and there is little doubt that it is television that has played the largest part in making the sport popular with such a large section of the community today, the majority of whom know little about horses.

But it is not only television; there are other reasons. First there is the simplicity of the rules, which makes for easy audience-understanding; it is no more difficult, in ninety-nine rounds out of a hundred, to judge a competition sitting in one's armchair at home, watching on television, than it is actually in the judges' box. A horse either hits a fence or it does not; it either jumps the fence or it stops. The rules, as already described, are for the most part simple. There are, of course, technicalities, but these seldom come into the picture. In the jump-off it is the fastest round that wins, if two horses have an equal number of faults, or

140

no faults at all; and as a rule, even on television, the clock can be clearly seen, often being superimposed on the picture.

Secondly, it is a clean sport. For reasons already given, prize money is all-important, and therefore everyone competing wants to win; there is no 'doping' or 'pulling' or jiggery-pokery of any sort; every horse that enters the arena comes in to win, and as a result the public knows just where it is. Betting is, in fact, not illegal in show jumping but, although it has been tried, it has never caught on, which is probably an excellent thing. As dealt with in the chapter on accusations of cruelty, it may be that from time to time one is unfortunate enough to see a horse that has been 'rapped' or in some way frightened into jumping well, but this is a rarity and, for the most part, such incidents are unknown to the audience.

The atmosphere surrounding show-jumping is a very sporting one; this is because, although each rider is anxious to win any particular competition, nevertheless there is not cut-throat competition between them; the leading show jumping riders are a cheerful, generous crowd; they are delighted to see a win for someone who has shown particular skill or courage. Obviously it can be disappointing if one is leading in a jump-off against the clock, and then another rider comes in and takes a risk that one would not have dared to take oneself, gets away with it, and clips a second or two off one's leading time. Nevertheless, such skills are admired by the riders, who know only too well the problems involved.

I remember, recently, the immense delight of all the riders when a popular rider who had been out of luck for a year or two —not having the best horses, seldom winning a big competition —pulled off a really major victory in one of the most important competitions at the Horse of the Year Show. None cheered louder than this rider's opponents.

This generous, cheerful attitude existing between the riders communicates itself to the audience, and, consequently, the sport is invariably surrounded by a happy, as well as an excited, atmosphere.

Nor should one forget the part played by the horse itself.

POPULARITY OF SHOW JUMPING

There is, deep down in most British people, an innate affection for the horse. This is largely because it is only a generation or two back that everybody in these islands was working with, and using, horses; there was no other means of transport: the motor car had not been invented. Anyone who has worked with horses has an affection for them. There are many reasons for this—many of them too complex to deal with in this particular book—but the fact remains that, in most people, there is, deep down, a love of horses. It is partly, of course, aesthetic; the horse is a magnificent and beautiful creature to look at, as, from the very earliest days, every sculptor, and many poets, have discovered for themselves.

On television, perhaps, the horse looks even more glamorous; he is undoubtedly 'tele-photogenic' and the sight of him galloping, jumping big fences, with all his power and strength and elegance, is bound to cause an elated reaction in the average person.

But it is more than this; the horse is known as the friend and servant of Man, and at least part of his popularity lies in the fact that he is so willing to serve Man in many different ways —usually quite uncomplainingly—while, at the same time, taking no advantage of his immense, superior strength.

It is, perhaps, worth quoting here the very fine tribute to the horse which is recited at the end of each Horse of the Year Show—the final climax of the show jumping season in Britain; these lines were, in fact, specially written to be used by myself, as the Horse Show commentator, at the end of the Show, by Ronald Duncan—a West Country farmer, but also an eminent playwright and poet. It goes without saying that he is also a great lover of the horse.

At the end of the Show, when the final prizes have been presented, there is a great cavalcade of all the leading horses, ponies and riders connected with the Show, until the arena is full of more than one hundred animals. The trumpeters of the Household Cavalry, on their splendid grey horses and in their magnificent uniforms, sound a final fanfare. This is followed by what always seems to me to be an astonishing silence remembering that more than a hundred horses and ponies are crammed in that arena, and nearly ten thousand people are crammed in the seats of the stadium; yet, in fact, the silence is complete save for the possible jingle of a bit, the clink of a spur, or the impatient snort of a horse as he paws the tan. It is then that the tribute is recited, giving thanks as it does for all the pleasure that horses can still give us—even in this highly mechanized age.

'Where in this wide world can man find nobility without pride, friendship without envy, or beauty without vanity? Here, where grace is laced with muscle and strength by gentleness confined.

'He serves without servility; he has fought without enmity. There is nothing so powerful, nothing less violent; there is nothing so quick, nothing more patient.

'England's past has been borne on his back. All our history is his industry. We are his heirs; he our inheritance:

—THE HORSE!'

It cannot possibly be denied, however, that it is, more than anything else, television that has really made show jumping. It is one of the few fortunate sports that has benefited from television, in that it has introduced to the sport a large new audience, but has not succeeded in reducing the 'gate'. It is difficult to say whether the smaller show suffers because people have become blasé and are disappointed at not seeing all the stars that they have seen on television, or whether it gains because people have seen Marion Coakes or Harvey Smith or David Broome or Alan Oliver on television, hear that he or she is jumping at the local show, and go along to see for themselves—something that they would never have thought of doing twenty years ago. It is obvious that many people will stay at home and watch television, the coverage of most big shows being outstandingly good, rather than make the effort to go to the show itself; but the number of such people is offset by those whose interest has been awakened by television and feel that they must go along and see for themselves, and then, having gone once, find themselves caught in the spell, and become regulars.

POPULARITY OF SHOW JUMPING

It is interesting that, at the Horse of the Year Show, which is an indoor show with a limited number of seats, the evening performances are always crowded out because, to get in, seats have to be booked in advance. All seats for the last two performances of the Show, which takes place in October, are booked out in April and, during the actual Show, touts are selling £1 tickets for as much as £10. At the White City, however, for the Royal International Horse Show, it was perhaps only on the Wednesday night, the big night when the King George V Cup—generally considered the most important individual championship in the world—was competed for (usually in the presence of the Queen), that it was difficult to get in. The White City Stadium had obviously a much greater capacity, but it was more than this; it was most noticeable how, if the weather was bad at 5 or 6 o'clock in the late afternoon, the unreserved seats were empty later that evening. People felt that it was going to be wet and cold, and so stayed at home and watched it on the television. If, on the other hand, it was fine at that time, then the crowds rolled up, suggesting that many people, rightly and understandably, prefer to be there themselves with all the colour and the atmosphere rather than to have it second-hand on television. There is, in fact, another reason for show jumping being successful on television. This could be called a technical reason—certainly it is one that is not usually appreciated.

In show jumping everything that matters is contained on the screen, and there are only three things that matter: the horse, the rider and the fence. All these can be seen clearly, often closely, on television; this helps to rivet the attention of the viewer and, because he is seeing everything that matters, he is becoming involved. More than that, he is less willing to allow himself to be distracted. Most important of all, he can still, although his knowledge of the sport is limited, understand it because he can see everything that matters for himself.

There are very few sports to which this applies and those to which it does are invariably the most popular sports on television—not necessarily amongst the *cognoscenti* of that sport, but also amongst the lay public. The obvious examples are

144

17a & b. Leading Ladies I. Althea Roger Smith winner of the 1966 Queen Elizabeth Cup on Havana Royal, and (*below*) Anneli Drummond Hay on Merely-a-Monarch.

18a & b. Leading Ladies II. Jean Goodwin, Ladies National Champion on Hobo in 1966, and (*below*) Caroline Bradley, winner of two competitions at her first international horse show, Dublin 1965.

boxing, wrestling, tennis; everything that matters can be clearly seen by the viewing audience. In football it is not always possible to know what part of the ground is being televised at any precise moment—a viewer can see a long pass by the centre forward, but he cannot immediately see whether there is anyone on the wing to receive that pass. In cricket, a batsman can turn a ball sharply round to long leg, but the viewer does not know whether there is a fielder on the leg boundary or whether that ball is going for four. In racing, the likelihood, is that, after a few furlongs, the field is so spread out that it cannot possibly be covered by one camera; the producer, therefore, has to decide whether to keep his camera on the one horse that is right out in front or on the body of the field, which may be ten lengths behind the leader. The viewer does not know how far they are behind, or even if there is a horse in front at all! The one thing that can be certain is that the horse in which he is interested in is not in the picture! This is likely to happen in any kind of racing.

Because of this incompleteness of the picture the non-involved viewer can easily allow his mind to wander and, after a time, he will feel completely detached, and not care particularly whether he carries on watching or not; whereas, if everything that matters is contained in the picture, he finds himself unexpectedly involved and does not want to stop watching.

I have no doubt that this is an important explanation of why show jumping is so popular on television. Often I am told so—indeed, get many hundreds of letters from viewers, who say that they are quite exhausted by the end of a programme of jumping, as they feel as if they have jumped every fence with every horse! They have found it sometimes unbearably exciting in a jump-off against the clock, or in a puissance competition, where there are only a few fences but they go up to a height possibly exceeding 7 ft. In other words, they have become involved.

The result of this is that they know the names of the horses and riders intimately and these horses and riders have become national stars. Any sport, if it is to be successful, needs stars—names that can draw a crowd: names to set people talking when they succeed or when they fail. In show jumping there is perhaps almost an *embarras de richesse* because 'when everyone is somebody, then no one's anybody'. Twenty years ago there were only, to all intents and purposes, Harry Llewellyn and Pat Smythe—Foxhunter and Tosca, though a few years later Nizefella, Craven A and others were to become almost equally popular. Today the strength of British show jumping is such that we have, perhaps, as many as two dozen riders and horses competent to represent Britain in international competition; it is significant that, both times we won the President's Cup— virtually the world championship, for it goes to the nation that has won the most points in international team jumping—no less than sixteen different riders represented Britain in international events. This means to say that, instead of two or three stars, we have some eighteen or twenty, which necessarily reduces the value of any one particular star, as it did in films when Charlie Chaplin and Greta Garbo, who for years had the field to themselves, suddenly found that every studio was producing a new star of its own, the value of their own coin being inevitably reduced.

With show jumping, however, this is less of a disadvantage in that, having so many horse shows in Britain during the season—at least two thousand—it is necessary to have enough stars to go round and, although of course they all meet at the really big shows, such as Windsor, the Royal, the International and the Horse of the Year Show, at the majority of the big county shows there are at least three or four names that have become familiar through television; which helps to draw the crowd and hold the interest of the spectators.

CHAPTER XIII

The Future of Show Jumping

Show jumping today is in a very healthy state and one hopes that it will continue to be so for many years to come, but other sports—even the most popular, even those considered to be the most national of all our sports—have had their bad patches, and it could, of course, happen to show jumping.

Fortunately, show jumping is an extremely well-organized sport; this is largely due to the organization set up by Sir Mike Ansell twenty years ago, and improved constantly and modernized, thanks entirely to his own genius and the support, advice and assistance from an extremely able committee. As long as the conduct of show jumping is in the hands of these people the future must seem to be reasonably secure.

Nevertheless, trends change; fashions change. The public is notoriously fickle and, if show jumping is to continue to be as popular as it is at present, then obviously one must be forewarned and forearmed against any of those eventualities that might lead to its loss of popularity.

Although people who are most interested, most closely concerned, with show jumping at a comparatively humble level—Foxhunter competitions and so on—may resent this, it is nevertheless a fact that the success of show jumping hinges very largely on the success of our jumpers in the international sphere. When our riders are successful competing against famous riders of other nations, and showing that they are their equals if not their superiors, then they become well known to a far wider public than just those people who are interested in horses; this is a great help as far as attendances at the shows are concerned (which, indirectly, as previously experienced, helps the finances of show jumping); but, more than that, it is a stimulus to young and to new riders. It ensures that there are plenty of riding members of the Association who will see to it that the classes in the shows held all over the country are well filled; this, in turn, ensures a reliable reservoir of up and coming riders who will be able to take the places of the established stars of the present time.

It is sometimes suggested that too much money is spent on sending teams to compete in international shows abroad, but it must be remembered that this money is collected and is given in subscriptions and donations, and none of the cost, therefore, of sending teams abroad falls directly on the sport.

There can be no doubt whatever that to succeed internationally is of paramount importance in the whole success and the future success of show jumping.

Naturally—indeed, it has already been suggested—the leading riders become household names, but it will be fatal for the sport if they ever allow themselves to become *prima donnas*; any sport that has been run by the performers themselves has got into difficulties. Obviously it is not easy for young riders who suddenly find themselves household names to avoid having their heads turned, to a greater or lesser extent. Fortunately, in show jumping, it is usually to a lesser extent because, in the first place these riders realize how much they owe to their horses; in the second place, their very background suggests that they are simple, natural people—not likely to allow success to go too much to their heads.

Nevertheless it is vitally important that our leading riders should not start dictating to the organizers—either at local level or national level. The organizers have the riders' interests closely at heart, and spend much time and energy in seeing that the sport is run to the greatest advantage to those who perform it. They are fully conscious of the importance of the riders themselves; nevertheless they know, too, that, from their position of detachment and integrity, it is essential that they should administer the sport rather than those taking part in it.

THE FUTURE OF SHOW JUMPING

It can only be harmful to the sport when one hears of a rider saying that he or she refuses to take part unless so-and-so builds the course, or argues the decision of a judge, or in any way makes a scene in public; the more sportsmanlike the riders can appear to be to the general public, the greater affection the public will have for their sport.

It has, too, to be appreciated that the rider today comes from a somewhat different background from the riders who first made the sport popular and famous. In the early days it was such as Col. Harry Llewellyn, Mr. Ruby Holland-Martin, Brigadier 'Monkey' Blacker, and, of course, Pat Smythe. Though it is not entirely the case with the latter—a unique rags-to-riches story, if ever there was one—the others, and many like them, were people of independent means. Many of them were retired Army officers; some of them were landed gentry. The prize money was of no great importance to them. What *was* important was to win for Britain; to improve the standard of British riders so that they were capable of taking on the best on the Continent.

Today it is rather different. Those taking part come from a much wider background; there is, perhaps, a majority of farmers and farmers' sons, many of whom pay more attention to the horses on their farms than any other stock. One might almost say that, indirectly, they were horse dealers; and there is nothing shameful in that. Leading riders today include a young man who runs a service station, a bricklayer, a car hire driver; others are the sons of prosperous businessmen, who look upon show jumping as an investment. It is, perhaps, only the girls who come from a less commercial background, though none of these could be described as social butterflies.

That the type of person enjoying the sport today is so different from the type who was show jumping fifteen years ago is quite immaterial; it is, in fact, basically advantageous to the sport; but not surprisingly the present-day riders are tougher, more concerned with winning, more anxious in getting good prize money, and of necessity desirous of selling their horses for good prices. All this is quite above board; things only go wrong if the commercial element is allowed to intrude to too great an extent, that the need to win becomes more important than the sport itself. This can only lead to people risking behaviour and practice that will be discreditable to the sport.

It has been said that the big prize money has been detrimental to the sport, but remembering that show jumping is essentially a spectator sport, that demands a high standard of performance to satisfy the spectators, obviously it is essential that good prize money should be offered to attract the best riders, including riders from overseas. This can only be produced by generous sponsors, many of whom only expect the smallest gains from the money they put forward in sponsoring a jumping competition. Others of course, understandably, expect the most they can get.

Although the prize money is big it should, however, be remembered that only some fifteen or twenty riders win as much as £1,000 in a single season.

It cannot possibly be denied that television has put show jumping 'on the map'. It is a sport that has, fortunately, gained more than it has lost by television coverage, because it has been introduced to a huge lay public to such an extent that it is true to say today that over 80 per cent of the people who enjoy show jumping, either on television or at a local show, have nothing whatever to do with horses.

Television is essential to show jumping, but it is also essential that show jumping should be properly presented on television. Being intimately concerned myself, I know of the immense amount of trouble that is taken in the arrangements made between the BBC and the British Horse Society and the British Show Jumping Association, to ensure that the very best jumping is seen by the viewers from the Royal International Horse Show at the White City and the Horse of the Year Show at Wembley. Endless trouble is taken over the timing of the competitions, so that the minimum amount of under-running or over-running is likely.

Through the years the BBC has co-operated to the full in this, accepting the word of the organizers that they will try to the very limit of their ability to see that, while the show is being televised, television will get the very best jumping.

THE FUTURE OF SHOW JUMPING

If—and this must always be considered a possibility—television, for one reason or another, lost interest in show jumping and was content to produce it shoddily, without sufficient attention being paid to the timing, so that viewers could not be assured of getting the result, which, after all, is the vital moment in any show competition, then very quickly the viewers would drift away. As it is at present there are figures to show that, whenever the big jumping is on, from the International Horse Show or from the Horse of the Year Show or from the Olympic Games or a big international competition, there is a drain from the Independent Television to BBC of anything up to a million and a half viewers.

Show jumping is grateful for this presentation and appreciates how much it owes to it. It appreciates, too, that without it the future could be very much less secure.

It is, perhaps, a pity that so often the Independent Television companies put on, during afternoon periods, long and sometimes not very interesting competitions which tend to leave viewers bored; the result of this could be that viewers imagine that all show jumping is boring forgetting that they have, in fact, only been watching a somewhat limited national competition, whereas television thrives on the big international occasion.

It must be said, too, that the success and popularity of show jumping must depend to a certain extent on Press coverage. Unfortunately the national Press does not feel inclined to give very much space to show jumping and, though perhaps they would not be prepared to admit it, there can be no doubt that the Press has the power to make or to break a sport. There have been plenty of examples of this during the last few years, when a comparatively new sport has been promoted by a national newspaper so that, within a few months, it has become a nationally popular sport.

A few of the major national papers do now have a Special Correspondent who gives coverage to the major shows. Unfortunately, however, so often the papers ignore the international shows taking place on the Continent—frequently the shows at which our riders are particularly distinguishing themselves, and therefore reminding readers that show jumping is a sport at which the British excel. British success gets no mention at all, or at best a couple of lines from Associated Press or Reuters, which are only likely to be found in an obscure corner, by those who are particularly looking for them.

This is unfortunate because so often it is these off-season successes that can do most to build up the image of show jumping, and the success that British riders enjoy in it.

As far as the general public is concerned it is unfortunately true to say that show jumping still has something of the image of a sport for the 'idle rich'. Indeed, horse riding in any form has this image, and it seems to be extraordinarily difficult to alter it, despite all the evidence that riding—and show jumping in particular—are enjoyed now by as wide a cross-section of the community as any other sport, and indeed, as far as show jumping is concerned, has a smaller number of wealthy or privileged people taking part than in any of the sports that seem to attract the Press and general public, such as golf, sailing, fishing.

It goes without saying that were the country to suffer a fatal economic crisis, any sport connected with horses, including show jumping, would inevitably suffer. It is possible, even, that if Britain joins the Common Market there will be increased problems because of the anticipated increases in food stuffs. But all sport will suffer from an economic crisis, and it would be wrong to pretend that show jumping is all that much more vulnerable than other sports. Obviously it is a 'luxury' sport, but in fact, what sport is not?

To sum up, the future of show jumping depends firstly on international success, secondly upon the behaviour and performance of those that take part in it and, thirdly, on the co-operation of television and newspapers. Given these, with the high standard of its organization, the simplicity and straightforwardness of its rules, and the sportsmanship of the riders and owners, there is no reason why show jumping should not continue to enjoy for many years the popularity and the success that it does at present.

CHAPTER XIV

Personally Speaking

I am often asked how I became so closely associated with show jumping, and what led me to becoming a commentator. The story is simple and quite straightforward.

I have told in the first chapter how my father was one of the original founders of the B.S.J.A. in the early 'twenties; for forty years after that he retained a close interest in their affairs—particularly on the administrative side; there was, therefore, a family connection.

It was, of course, this family connection that led to my getting into show jumping 'on the ground floor' for, in the early days of the B.S.J.A., there were not sufficient funds to employ a full-time secretary; my father, therefore, thought that it would be a convenient and happy solution if the nursery governess that my mother had recently employed to teach me and my brother and sister to read and write was also used as a part-time secretary to the B.S.J.A. (Hence far more of her time being taken up in addressing envelopes and distributing brochures than in teaching!)

When the financial crash came in the early 'thirties it led to the disposal of all our horses, which meant that I only did a very limited amount of practical show jumping myself in the years before the war, but long associated with teaching and having at one time received training in voice production it was understandable, particularly in view of my horsey connections, that I was invited to do the public address commentary shortly after the war at a show organized in the West Country. Knowing most of the riders and something of the problems facing them,

153

I was able to give a fairly lively and factual commentary, and this led to my being invited to do the commentary at the first International Horse Show held at the White City in 1947.

My brief on that occasion was to make the show jumping as interesting as possible to a lay public, because the B.S.J.A. and the British Horse Society were determined that this newly-revived show in London should have an appeal to the general public and not exist just for an exclusive minority as Olympia had. Accordingly, I took the trouble to acquaint myself with as much detail as possible about all the riders and horses taking part.

These numbered several hundred, and it was necessary, therefore, for me to start a card index system whereby I could turn up in a moment the card of any horse or rider and then inform the public of something of its background and its history.

This did seem to awaken a certain general interest and, allied with a certain knowledge about rules, courses and so on, which, again because of my background, I had at my fingertips, it was possible to involve the ordinary public a good deal more than hitherto.

The card index system, simple and obvious as it is, has been imitated by most commentators who do this sort of work seriously; though, in fact, I now seldom use it because, being familiar with the horses and riders, there are only the new names to absorb each season. The difficult problem, of course, is at the big international horse shows, when one has to seek out information about the foreign riders, and try to memorize it. As a rule, I still use cards for these.

When show jumping was televised for the first time—the actual first transmission of a show jumping competition was the 1948 Olympic Games at Wembley—it was obvious that the public address commentary would have to be incorporated into the television commentary. This was because, firstly, there was not time, after the P.A. announcement, for the television commentator to give the public the sort of information it wanted before the rider had started on his round and, secondly, because the television commentator, expert as he was as a commentator

—it was, in fact, in these early days, Peter Dimmock himself—knew little about show jumping and those who performed in it.

When after two or three years television began seriously to cover show jumping, I was invited to become a television commentator, I believed that, in some way, the task would be easier if I combined both the television commentary and the public address commentary. This, in fact, is far less difficult than it might appear to be. In the first place, the television commentator has earphones on and it is difficult, therefore, to hear what the public address commentator is saying; there is always, consequently, a possibility that the television commentator will either repeat or contradict something that has just been said over the public address, which, of course is irritating to viewers. A greater problem, however, is that the television commentator does not know when the public address commentator is going to start speaking; obviously, they cannot both speak at the same time and therefore, frequently, the television commentator finds himself having to break off in mid-sentence. This obviously, is bad television.

By doing the two (and it simply means using two microphones, which admittedly can, very occasionally, lead to the commentator speaking into the wrong microphone—and it has happened!) the commentator is able to make his two commentaries complementary; this results in a considerable reduction in the amount of talking and it must always be remembered that the real virtue of a good commentator is how much he does *not* talk.

This applies particularly to television because, of course, the viewer is perfectly capable, nine times out of ten, of seeing for himself.

The technique that I attempt to follow is to do the greater part of the talking at the beginning of the programme, setting the scene, explaining what sort of competition it is, telling the audience of the number of clear rounds, who has fallen by the wayside and so on, and then gradually speaking less, and less —and less! So that, eventually, it is necessary to say no more than the horse's name, and let the picture tell the rest of the story, the only comment from the commentator being, perhaps, an intake of breath or an exclamation which is, in fact, reflecting the feelings of the spectators actually present.

I believe very firmly that it is part of the commentator's job to convey to the viewers something of the atmosphere of the occasion, the tension at the ringside; for this reason I have always refused to do my commentaries from a soundproof glass box, as one is then entirely divorced from the atmosphere of the arena. At the International I actually do my commentary from the centre of the ring; the control point of the show. At the Horse of the Year Show I sit right by the ring-side—again at the control point; in this way I feel that I am able to communicate something of the excitement and interest of the spectators present, to the viewers in their homes.

There is nothing very difficult about commentating, as long as one knows intimately the sport upon which one is commentating. Viewers can tell very quickly if a commentator is 'flannelling' because a commentator only does this when he is not very conversant with the sport he is talking about; it is then, invariably, that he talks too much, whereas the commentator who really knows his sport knows the language, the phrases that are usually employed, the vernacular, can reduce his commentary to a minimum.

It is an interesting fact that, although the number of experts in any viewing audience is always small, yet it is not only they but the lay public as well, who appreciate immediately if a commentator is not properly conversant with his sport.

When I first started broadcasting, Peter Dimmock gave me some admirable advice—'When in doubt, say nowt!' The viewing audience never minds if the commentator is silent. The real art of the commentator is to be a whisper over the shoulder explaining something just before the viewer has time to ask the question. The key word in all commentating is 'identify'. A commentator must never speak about something that the viewers cannot see; this very quickly irritates and leads to the viewer losing interest.

Once the programme is thoroughly launched the picture can tell nine-tenths of the story and the commentator should appreciate this; it is irritating to viewers if the commentator keeps saying the obvious.

Often one is asked if one does not get a sore throat from doing so much talking. Apart from the fact that one should not 'do so much talking', there is never any reason why the throat should get sore because, speaking into a microphone, one is using the minimum of voice. It is, however, a matter of extremely tense concentration, and this, of course, can be very exhausting.

Inevitably, as far as the general public is concerned, because one is so much associated with horses they imagine one to be half a horse! In fact horses are, for me, a hobby, and broadcasting very much a part-time employment, but I have to admit that my lifelong connection with horses, with education and my preoccupation with the production of plays, pageants and so on —which, leads to a great deal of reading, a certain amount of lecturing and a considerable amount of writing—have all of course, helped me a great deal in the techniques of broadcasting.

As a commentator I quite simply look upon it as my job to communicate in an accurate and interesting manner, to the large lay public something, of my own interest and enthusiasm for this great sport.

Principal Results During the last Ten Years

OLYMPIC GAMES

1948 LONDON
Team: 1. Mexico; 2. Spain; 3. Gt. Britain (Lt.-Col. H. M. Llewellyn's Foxhunter, Lt.-Col. H. M. V. Nicholl's Kilgeddin and Major A. Carr's Monty).
Individual: 1. Col. H. Mariles Cortes on Arete (Mexico): 2. Capt. R. Uriza on Hatuey (Mexico); 3. J. F. M. d'Orgeix on Sucre de Pomme (France).

1952 HELSINKI
Team: 1. Great Britain (Lt.-Col. H. M. Llewellyn's Foxhunter, W. H. White's Nizefela and Col. D. N. Stewart on Aherlow); 2. Chile; 3. U.S.A.
Individual: 1. P. J. d'Oriola's Ali Baba (France); 2. Major O. Cristi's Bambi (Chile); F. Theidemann's Meteor (Germany).

1956 STOCKHOLM
Team: 1, Germany; 2. Italy; 3. Great Britain (Miss P. Smythe on Flanagan, W. H. White on Nizefela and P. Robeson on Schorchin').
Individual: 1. H. G. Winkler's Halla (Germany); Capt. R. d'Inzeo on Merano (Italy); 3. Capt. P. d'Inzeo on Uruguay (Italy).

1960 ROME
Team: 1. Germany; 2. U.S.A.; 3. Italy.

PRINCIPAL RESULTS

Individual: 1. Capt. R. d'Inzeo on Posillipo (Italy); Capt. P. d'Inzeo on The Rock (Italy); 3. D. Broome on O. Anderson's Sunsalve (G.B.).

1964 TOKYO

Team: 1. Germany; 2. France; 3. Italy; 4. Great Britain. *Individual:* 1. P. J. d'Oriola on Lutteur B. (France); 2. H. Schridde on Dozent II (Germany); 3. P. Robeson on Firecrest (G.B.).

ROYAL INTERNATIONAL HORSE SHOW

KING GEORGE V CUP

1958. H. Wiley on Master William (U.S.A.)
1959. H. Wiley on Nautical (U.S.A.)
1960. D. Broome on Sunsalve (G.B.)
1961. Capt. P. d'Inzeo on The Rock (Italy)
1962. Capt. P. d'Inzeo on The Rock (Italy).
1963. T. Wade on Dundrum (Eire).
1964. W. Steinkraus on Sinjon (U.S.A.).
1965. H. G. Winkler on Fortun (Germany).
1966. D. Broome on Mister Softee (G.B.)
1967. P. Robeson on Firecrest (G.B.).

LONSDALE PUISSANCE CHAMPIONSHIP

1958. Capt. P. d'Inzeo on The Rock (Italy).
1959. Mrs. W. Wofford on Hallandia and Miss A. Townsend on Bandit IV (both G.B.).
1960. W. Steinkraus on Ksar d'Esprit (U.S.A.).
1961. N. Pessoa on Gran Geste (Brazil).
1962. K. Jarasinski on Raffaela (Germany).
1963. H. Möhr on Troll (Switzerland).
1964 Miss E. Broome on T. H. Edgar's Jacopo (G.B.).
1965. Miss A. Westwood on The Maverick and F. Welch on Brule Tout (both G.B.).
1966. Miss J. Goodwin on Sky Rocket (G.B.).

PRINCIPAL RESULTS

1967. H. Smith on Harvester (G.B.) and S. Hayes on Goodbye (Eire).

Daily Mail Championship
1958. Capt. P. d'Inzeo on Uruguay (Italy).
1959. H. Wiley on Nautical (U.S.A.).
1960. Miss P. Smythe on Scorchin' (G.B.).
1961. G. Mancinelli on Rockette (Italy).
1962. Miss P. Smythe on Scorchin' (G.B.).
1963. Miss A. Townsend on Dunboyne (G.B.).
1964. P. Robeson on Firecrest (G.B.).
1965. S. Hayes on Goodbye (Eire).
1966. Capt. W. Ringrose on Lough an Easpaig (Eire).
1967. G. Mancinelli on Petter Patter (Italy).

Queen Elizabeth II Cup
1958. Miss P. Smythe on Mr. Pollard (G.B.).
1959. Frl. Anna Clement on Nico (Germany).
1960. Miss S. Cohen on Clare Castle (G.B.).
1961. Lady S. Fitzalan Howard on Oorskiet (G.B.)
1962. Mrs. B. J. Crago on Spring Fever (G.B.).
1963. Miss J. Nash on Trigger Hill (G.B.).
1964. Miss G. M. Makin on Jubilant (G.B.).
1965. Miss M. Coakes on Stroller (G.B.).
1966. Miss A. Roger Smith on Havana Royal (G.B.).
1967. Miss B. Jennaway on Greyleg (G.B.).

IRISH TROPHY (GRAND PRIX) DUBLIN

1958. G. Morris on Night Owl (U.S.A.).
1959. S. Hayes on Kilrush (Eire).
1960. D. Broome on Sunsalve (G.B.).
1961. T. Wade on Dundrum (Eire).
1962. Capt. P. d'Inzeo on The Rock (Italy).
1963. T. Wade on Dundrum (Eire).
1964. Miss K. Kusner on Untouchable (U.S.A.).

PRINCIPAL RESULTS

1965. Miss K. Kusner on Untouchable (U.S.A.).
1966. Hon. D. Connolly Carew on Barrymore (Eire).
1967. S. Hayes on Ramona (Eire).

HORSE OF THE YEAR SHOW
Leading Show Jumper of the Year

1958. T. H. Edgar on Jane Summers and Miss P. Smythe on Mr. Pollard.
1959. H. Smith on Farmer's Boy.
1960. T. Williams on Pegasus XIII.
1961. D. B. Barker on Lucky Sam and Miss C. Beard on Mayfly.
1962. Miss P. Smythe on Flanagan.
1963. A. Fielder on Vibart.
1964. Mrs. C. D. Barker on Atalanta.
1965. H. Smith on Warpaint.
1966. A. Fielder on Vibart.
1967. H. Smith on Harvester.

B.S.J.A. NATIONAL CHAMPIONSHIP

1958. P. McMahon on Tim II.
1959. A. Oliver on John Gilpin.
1960. H. Smith on Farmer's Boy.
1961. D. Broome on Discutido.
1962. D. Broome on Wildfire.
1963. H. Smith on O'Malley.
1964. Miss E. Broome on T. H. Edgar's Jacopo.
1965. P. Robeson on Firecrest.
1966. A. Fielder on Vibart.
1967. D. Broome on Mister Softee.

PRINCIPAL RESULTS

LEADING HORSES
(assessed on prize money)

1958. Ted Williams on Pegasus XIII.
1959. D. Broome on Wildfire.
1960. Ted Williams on Pegasus XIII (for fifth time).
1961. D. Broome on Discutido.
1962. D. Broome on Wildfire.
1963. H. Smith on O'Malley.
1964. H. Smith on O'Malley.
1965. H. Smith on Harvester.
1966. D. Broome on Mister Softee.
1967. H. Smith on Harvester.

BRITISH JUMPING DERBY AT HICKSTEAD

1961. S. Hayes on Goodbye (Eire).
1962. Miss P. Smythe on Flanagan (G.B.).
1963. N. Pessoa on Gran Geste (Brazil).
1964. S. Hayes on Goodbye (Eire).
1965. N. Pessoa on Gran Geste (Brazil).
1966. D. Broome on Mister Softee (G.B.).
1967. Miss M. Coakes on Stroller (G.B.).

162